WHEN IS BUDDY COMING HOME?

ALSO BY GARY KURZ

Cold Noses at the Pearly Gates

Wagging Tails in Heaven

Furry Friends Forevermore

WHEN IS BUDDY COMING HOME?

A Parent's Guide to Helping
Your Child with the Loss of a Pet

GARY KURZ

CITADEL PRESS
Kensington Publishing Corp.
www.kensingtonbooks.com

CITADEL PRESS BOOKS are published by

Kensington Publishing Corp.
119 West 40th Street
New York, NY 10018

All Kensington titles, imprints, and distributed lines are available at special quantity discounts for bulk purchases for sales promotions, premiums, fund-raising, educational, or institutional use. Special book excerpts or customized printings can also be created to fit specific needs. For details, write or phone the office of the Kensington sales manager: Kensington Publishing Corp., 119 West 40th Street, New York, NY 10018, attn: Sales Department; phone 1-800-221-2647.

CITADEL PRESS and the Citadel logo are Reg. U.S. Pat. & TM Off.

ISBN-13: 978-0-8065-3817-4
ISBN-10: 0-8065-3817-1

First printing: June 2017

10 9 8 7 6 5 4 3 2 1

Printed in the United States of America

Library of Congress CIP data is available.

First electronic edition: June 2017

ISBN-13: 978-0-8065-3818-1
ISBN-10: 0-8065-3818-X

Contents

Foreword

Often it is the unusual that brings people together, forging friendships that grow more dear as time passes. In some cases, it is personal tragedy that initiates that friendship. When that happens, the friendship becomes bittersweet. It is the tragedy that adds the dynamic that causes those individuals to meet, but it is also what bonds them together in a way that becomes more precious over time. That is how my friendship with the author of this book, Gary Kurz, began.

Through the loss of our precious pet, a long-haired Chihuahua named Blu, who was taken from us tragically and prematurely at the age of three, I became acquainted with Gary as I corresponded with him and began reading his books, *Cold Noses at the Pearly Gates* and *Wagging Tails in Heaven*.

For any of you who have a love for animals, and especially for those of us who have lost a pet, I don't have to tell you about the pain that comes with their passing. Nor do I feel I need to remind you how those who try to enter into that pain to help us often become precious, simply in the attempts they make to comfort us.

That is the preciousness that I found as I read this author's words. My family's grief became all-consuming and the pain overwhelming. Yet, in the words that fell from the pages of these books, we found someone who wrote from his own experience and shared his own pain. I personally felt that Gary was sitting in my home offering that help, and it felt as if I was talking to an old friend who had known me for years.

What I found in Gary's books were not only warmth and compassion for what we were experiencing, but the fact that his books are full of the comfort of the Bible. He believes it to be the inerrant Word of God. As an ordained, Bible-believing minister myself, I found that to be refreshing.

The subject of animal afterlife will always be a controversial one, but I am happy to report that Gary comes at it from the authority of the truth of God's Word. His conclusions are not contrived or forced. If he shares an opinion with you, he is quick to communicate that it is his opinion. But when he comes to what the Scriptures actually say, he will not compromise.

He not only believes the Bible; he also loves it. It is more than a tool for him; it is a love letter from God Himself. The attitude with which he has approached this subject was exactly what I needed at that time. I didn't want opinion, conjecture, or sentimentality. I needed the truth.

I found a friend in Gary who had been through the same loss I was going through, and I found in him a kindred spirit who understood the suffering I was going through as I combed through the Scriptures. As I read his words, I found there was much that Gary and I shared in common. If you are unfamiliar with Gary's books, or if you are someone who has never studied what the Bible says on this subject, I believe you will be surprised to discover that God has said more on the subject of the afterlife of animals than you might have previously thought.

One of the biggest helps that I think reading Gary's books will bring to readers is in the area of the consciousness of the soul after death as it relates to animals and in what state our beloved friends are after death. That part of the book was especially helpful to me. Gary writes and communicates as a minister of the gospel and with the precision of a biblical scholar, yet with a warmth that many lack when dealing with this delicate, yet necessary subject.

In this latest book, Gary writes for the next generation, offering assistance and guidance to parents and other caregivers of children in explaining the deaths of their pets and all the peripheral questions that children commonly ask. He offers parents insightful commentary and pertinent scripture references to help them give answers to the questions that only children can ask.

I recommend, without any hesitation or reservation, the book you are about to read. I truly believe the message the author shares in it can change your life. I have been privileged to write this foreword, and I do so in honor of my "best buddy," Blu, whom I love and miss every day. But I know I will one day see him again, because of the hope I have in Christ through the promises in His Word.

To this I add my prayers for you, that you will find in its pages the help and guidance you need. May you come to know, intimately, the Creator who loves you and who has provided a plan for each one of us as His creations, whether animal or human, and may you come to realize and fulfill that plan for His glory.

Thankfully,
Elbert Sorrel
Pastor

WHEN IS BUDDY COMING HOME?

INTRODUCTION

In homes where pets are allowed to coexist with people, more often than not, they are considered a very real part of the family. This status is not cliché; they are actually integral and important components of the family. They are loved, and frequently cherished.

If one were to define their role in conventional terms, the term *perpetual children* would seem appropriate. They are "children," because, like children, they depend upon their families to meet virtually all of their needs (i.e., food, shelter, safety, care, etc.).

And they are "perpetual," because they never leave the nest. Pets do not marry. They do not go off to college or join the military. Typically, they remain with the family for life, unable to fully care for themselves. Is it any wonder, then, that their passing, regardless of whether it was expected or not, has a similar impact upon the family as that of a human family member passing?

Indeed, the death of the family pet can be extremely traumatic and life-altering. Family members, collectively and individually, find themselves experiencing myriad reactions, oftentimes so unexpectedly overwhelming that it is difficult for them to function.

Finding the motivation to perform daily routines and responsibilities can prove to be very difficult. Solid, stable adults find themselves suddenly unable to work or concentrate, during at least the initial few days following the death of their "best friend."

Admittedly, reactions vary widely among adults, from mild grief and gentle weeping, up to and including the aforementioned emotional paralysis. Of course, reactions vary due to a number of factors. These may include: a person's closeness to the animal; their personal outlook on life and death; the need to appear upbeat around their children; the amount of social interaction their job requires of them during the initial period of grief; and even their religious beliefs, to name a few.

With children, however, the factors that are important to adults are not quite as important to them. Children's lives are much less complicated than the average adult's. They are not as concerned about social interactions or helping others cope with the pain. They only know that their hearts are broken, and they want to understand what has happened and what it all means to them.

When something suddenly changes in children's lives, it is emotionally unsettling and upsetting to them, especially when that change is the loss of someone they love, animal or human. The impact on their tender hearts can be very traumatic. Their only means of coping and regaining stability in their lives may be to look to parents for explanations and comfort.

One of the most heartbreaking aspects of my work as a pet

loss author is to hear from readers that they have been unable to help their children with their pain and grief. They lament that they have tried everything that they know to do, but without success. They are concerned that their children have lost the "spark" in their lives, and they confess that they do not know what to do to help them through the relentless sorrow they are experiencing.

As I alluded to earlier, it has been my experience that children simply want to understand this big change in their lives. They need answers to settle the turmoil they feel inside. When adults contact me for help with their own grief, they are simply looking for answers to the questions that haunt them. They want to know whether animals have souls, whether God has provided an afterlife for them or whether this life was all the life they will ever know. Why should we not expect that children have the same questions on their minds?

The problem is that many children either do not know how to ask these questions, or they simply do not want to. Perhaps they are embarrassed. Maybe they are afraid of what the answers might be. Whatever their reasoning, their silence does not mean they aren't bothered by the same tough questions that bother us adults.

This book is meant to be a quick reference guide for parents to help answer those questions. It is based upon my extensive personal studies and research and my many years of experience in the field of pet loss, including what I have learned from tens of thousands of readers who have corresponded with me about their losses and sorrow. If you suspect that your child needs professional assistance to cope with depression or anxiety, please seek out that help immediately.

This book is offered as a help for parents to respond to or approach their children with dependable, Bible-based answers that should prove to be uplifting and helpful. Not every child will have the same questions, but I think you will find that the most common concerns are addressed here.

Most of the chapters will contain the same simple format as indicated below:

- 🐾 A typical question that a child might ask is posed.
- 🐾 A scripture that relates to the question will be given.
- 🐾 A heartfelt analysis and explanation will be provided as it applies to the question. An illustration will also be provided when appropriate.
- 🐾 And finally, a simple suggested approach/narrative that parents can read or paraphrase to their child will be shared.

NOTE TO PARENTS

To preclude overuse of the words *he, she, him,* and *her,* I will be using an imaginary pet name throughout the book. I have randomly selected "Buddy" as that name. If that was your pet's name, I sincerely hope my use of it will not cause you any unnecessary pain or discomfort.

Chapter 1
"What is Death, Mommy?"

Well, that is an easy question to answer, isn't it? Death is simply the termination of all biological functions that sustain a living organism, right? Try that on your child when they need compassion and comfort. Have your camera ready, though, because the facial expressions they make will probably be quite memorable.

Death can be a scary topic for anyone, but especially for children!

Seriously, this will probably be one of the toughest questions you will ever be asked by your child, and you need to be prepared with a good answer. Unfortunately, several factors can make this question potentially more difficult to respond to. For one, you may anticipate that your child will not ask you about death until someone known to the family has actually passed away.

Don't kid yourself. Children are walking, talking question marks. They want to know about everything. And they are relentless in their quest for knowledge and understanding. The question about death might be prompted by something as simple as seeing a dead bird in the lawn or from watching a television program about hunting. But one thing we can be certain about: It will come when you least expect it. So, expect it!

Another factor that could aggravate or complicate the question is a generational issue. Today's children are so overexposed to artificial and "play" death on video and online games, movies, and even seemingly harmless cartoons, that their concept of death may be considerably warped.

At the lower end of the age scale, youngsters may view death as something temporary or reversible. All they have to do is hit the RESET button on their game and the hero is back in business. And in cartoons, characters who are squashed by falling rocks or pianos or who are blown up by invading aliens come back next week to do it all again.

Adults know the difference between imaginary and real. That a difference exists, however, doesn't even occur to many younger children. For older children, they may understand the difference, but they are so overexposed to death and carnage in the media or in their video games that it just doesn't hold as much dread or impact for them as it does for us older people.

From whatever the source, children usually are already acquainted with the idea of death before their parents ever begin thinking about discussing it with them. But again, their understanding may be off the mark, and parents need to be proactive in setting the record straight. There is no "official" matrix for how to approach the topic, and in my opinion, there ought not to be. Each child is different. Each parent is different. What works for one may not work for another. I am not offering a cookie-cutter approach, but am merely providing you with information that you can then adapt to your particular situation.

There are many places in the Bible that we could turn to for a definition and explanation of what death means to living things, but one that seems to fit best in this chapter is **Job 12:10**, which says:

> *In whose hand is the soul of every living thing,*
> *and the breath of all mankind.*

The first ten words of this passage are extremely profound. The initial, face-value perception is that God is speaking about all creatures, human and animal. So there is no doubt, if one were to complete an in-depth study of this passage, the conclusion would yield the same result: that God is, indeed, speaking about all creatures, not just humans.

The word *soul* is used in over twenty different ways in the Bible. Invariably, when people come across this word in the Scriptures, they automatically associate it with other uses of similar words that speak to redemption. This happens so frequently that in no matter what context it appears, the connection to reconciliation and salvation is usually present in people's minds and unconsciously applied to the interpretation.

In most cases, this is right and acceptable to the rules of exegesis. But there are instances in which it is not. Clearly, the gospel message is not for animals. It is exclusively for people. It is a reconciliatory outreach from God to people.

However, to allow this truth to cause one to draw the conclusion that an animal therefore cannot have a soul is to visit a gross injustice on the Scriptures, in particular this verse, which has nothing to do with spiritual redemption.

*The word "soul" has many different
meanings in the Scriptures.*

The Hebrew word *nephesh* ("soul") is used in **Job 12:10**. It appears many times in the Scriptures and is used interchangeably to describe both the essence of man and of animals. It does not make a distinction between the two, and it does not delve into salvation in its application. Rather, it addresses the consciousness of the soul.

This passage in Job is a good example of this. The word *soul* is not used in relation to redemption, but rather the verse addresses God's providential care. A clearer meaning of this verse would be "in whose hand is the life or essence of every living thing . . ." God is speaking of that part of both humans and animals that contains, or houses, the "life" He has given to them, that part that departs the body when the body expires.

When we mesh these thoughts in **Job** with **Romans 8** and **Revelation 5:9–13**, to name a few corresponding passages, the meaning is clear. The life, or essence, of every living thing is in the eternal care of the One who created that life.

However, this word in Job indicates an even deeper thought for us to consider. We often refer to ourselves as a "flesh-and-blood body with a soul." This is not so. In keeping with the absolute intent of this word *nephesh*, man is a soul that has been placed in a flesh-and-blood body. The distinction is subtle, but it is huge in effect. We are not bodies with souls. We are souls with bodies.

And not only us, but because the same word is used to describe the essence of animals, it applies to them, as well. Most of us have been taught that animals do not have souls. Technically, that is correct. They do not *have* souls; they *are* souls, just like human beings are also souls inside physical bodies.

It is important to have this background knowledge when responding to the questions of children, especially today's children. They are smarter and more savvy than they were when I was a lad. Technology has significantly raised the bar on children's awareness. The educational community is even considering revamping the entire IQ exam to measure today's youth.

In keeping with this, my experience as a Sunday school teacher tells me that when speaking to children, you need to be clear. If you are not, you can expect a barrage of other questions as they try to clarify the issue on their own.

If you simply reply to the title question with, "Well, all things die," that comes across as ambiguous to a child. You can expect them to snap back, "Well, does that mean I am going to die?" or "Are you going to die, too, Mommy?"

Another pitfall to avoid is making God into a villain. Be careful when you invoke the Bible or God in your answers. It may seem innocent enough to answer your child's question about a departed relative like this: "Grandpa is with God now because God needed him more than we did." I think you may be asking for trouble with an answer like that. I am positive that the next words out of your child's mouth are going to be something like, "Will God need me more, too, someday?"

Not only will this concern of your child break your heart, but you now have opened another can of worms to deal with. What you might say instead, if you do want to include God in the answer, is, "Grandpa was very old and ready to move on to where he could be young and healthy again. I am sure that he is very happy to be with God now."

Don't get yourself in a fix; think ahead and be clear in what you say. You might even guide your child's thinking in another direction. For instance, you might answer in this way: "Death is something that happens to all living things. The old leaves to go to heaven, and the new takes its place. That is why animals and people have babies. And then the babies grow up and have babies, too. And then later we all meet again in heaven. Someday don't you want to have your own children?"

And then keep it simple. The old television show *Dennis the Menace* portrayed well the inquisitive nature of children. Dennis was always asking Mr. Wilson a question that led to another question, and then another, and so on.

Had Mr. Wilson been clear and simple in his answers, there wouldn't have been a show. When speaking about death, use the words *die*, *died*, and *death*. Avoid more complex words or euphemisms like *passed away* or *demise*. The former will result in a question like, "What did he pass away from?"

Communicating with children is not complicated. Keep it simple. Keep it clear. And above all, reassure the child with each of your answers. Don't be wishy-washy (i.e., "Well, I guess your kitty is in heaven," etc.). Try never to frame your answers so that there is any potential of putting doubt or distress in the child's mind. If you do not personally believe the kitty went to heaven (although I can assure you that it did), then try to avoid answering that question so directly. Find another way to reassure your child.

In providing a suggested response for you to give your child on this question, I am going to assume that the circumstances of your pet's passing were due to age or illness associated with age. More often than not, this is the reason for pet loss. If the passing of your pet was premature due to accident or injury, I am sure you will be able to adjust the answer to better reflect the circumstances.

What to Share with Your Child
QUESTION: *"What is death, Mommy?"*

Your child comes to you and asks the above question. Unless you already have something prepared, consider using the following as your response:

Honey, that is a very big question for a little girl (boy). But I am glad you asked me about it. I have been thinking about that, too, lately.

I am sure you notice that there are people of all different ages.

Some people are young, like you. We call people of your age "kids." Others are a little older and a little bigger. We call them teenagers. And when teenagers get older, they become adults. Everyone grows older each and every day. It is exciting to get older and to learn and do new things. We get to go to different schools and meet new people, drive cars and get jobs.

Every year people celebrate their birthdays, and that day is the day we say that they are a year older. Birthdays are fun, aren't they? Some older people have had a lot of birthdays in their long lives. And you can tell how old they are by all the candles on their cakes. Sometimes there are so many candles that the cake looks like it is on fire, doesn't it?

But as we get older and get to do all these new and exciting things, our bodies are also getting older, and we start to slow down a little. The older we get, the harder it is for us to do all the things we used to do, like running and jumping. After a while our bodies get so old that it just gets too hard to do anything and our bodies stop working and we die.

But death is not the end of our lives—just the end of our lives here on earth. The Bible tells us in **John 5:24:** "He that . . . believeth on him that sent me has everlasting life, and shall not come into condemnation, but is passed from death unto life."

That means that our lives never really end. We close our eyes here, but we open them there in that place we call heaven right away. That is exciting to know, because all we know about heaven tells us it is a wonderful place, where everyone gets along and everyone is happy.

The Bible tells us that no one has ever seen anything like what we will see in heaven. And we have seen some beautiful things here on earth, haven't we? But as beautiful as those places we saw here were, God tells us in the Bible that heaven will be much, much prettier.

And something else the Bible tells us is that animals will be there, too. Our Buddy will be there. In fact, he is there right now. Now, Buddy had a wonderful life here. He had so much fun living with us. Do you remember all the fun we all had together? But as happy as he was here, he is much happier where he is now.

Now our Buddy is young once more, and he will never get old again. He hasn't jumped and run fast in years, but today he is doing both. And he is happy. He gets to see God all the time. That must be something. I am so happy for him.

And it makes me happy to know that one day we will see him again. Doesn't that make you happy, too? I know you miss him, and I am sure he misses you, too. But I know you are happy that he is no longer old anymore.

How about if we pray right now and thank God for letting Buddy be in our lives, and ask Him to take care of Buddy for us for a while?

Chapter 2

"Is God Real, Mommy?"

I struggled with whether to include this question at all. It just does not seem necessary to me. I have taught thousands of children in both spiritual and secular settings in a variety of cultures, over a period of more than four decades, and I have never met a preteen child who did not believe in God. I have never even met one who straddled the fence on the topic. Indeed, it seems that children have no difficulty at all with faith. Their innocence has shielded them from the wickedness and woes of this world that often cause us to doubt that there is a God who is in control.

Still, I am sure that there must be a few exceptions to this rule somewhere, and I want to make sure you have an answer should your child present this question to you. Besides, you may be using this book to help a teenaged child with questions about God and faith. And I cannot deny that I have met quite a few teens who expressed doubt about God's existence: evidence that the ills of the world were beginning to impact them negatively. Isn't it sad how just a few years of exposure to the world can change a young person's outlook on God and faith?

Let's put faith aside for a moment and talk about spiritual awareness. I may take the long way around to get to my point, possibly taking a few rabbit trails, as well, but I think you will appreciate the observations and conclusions that I share with you. They should give you more information and tools to help you respond decisively to your child's questions. So please humor me for just a moment.

To begin, I don't think anyone can deny that there is a supernatural or a spiritual world apart from our present physical world. Every culture, every group of people, in every era of human history has acknowledged a spiritual presence of one sort or another. Even the most committed atheist will admit that there are happenings and experiences that occur in our world that do not belong to our world—things that simply cannot be explained away by science, nature, or logic. There is something inside each of us that gives us an awareness that there is something or someone "out there" beyond the realm of our own physical existence. We just seem to "know."

It is commonly believed that animals are aware of these presences, that they have a sixth sense that allows them to tune in to spiritual beings. Society has ascribed to animals an ability to perceive the supernatural in ways that humans cannot. There is no proof or explanation to support this widely accepted claim. It is just one of those urban legends that has gotten wheels and rolled along from generation to generation.

As a person who has been intimately involved with animals and nature his entire life, I do not personally subscribe to that view. I just do not see any evidence to support the notion that animals have a spiritual awareness. I won't go into detail here,

as I do that in other books I have written, and neither I nor readers appreciate redundancy. But I cannot take a position without
offering some proof, so I will offer a short example to support
my view on this matter.

During the demolition of a building, reporters were amazed
at how the many hundreds of pigeons that roosted in the building seemed to know to fly off just moments before the explo-
sives were detonated and the building came crumbling down.
They raved on and on about the "supernatural" ability of these
pigeons, and how all animals seem to know the future or to perceive upcoming danger.

Unfortunately, when the footage of the explosion was run in
slow motion, however, it became clear that the pigeons did not
take flight until almost a full second after the detonation. Their
sharp sense of touch and hearing were enough for them to hear
the sound and feel the shudder of the building before the effects
of the blast actually arrived at their position, allowing them the
opportunity to flee the danger before it was upon them.

We humans like to dwell on the sensational, and if it isn't sensational enough, we are quite willing to embellish a story. Everyone knows the psychological exercise in which one person is told
a story and then asked to pass it on to the next person, and so
on and so forth, until a dozen or more people have retold the
story. When the last person in the chain is asked to tell the story
out loud to the group, and their account is compared to the original, everyone gets a great laugh at how much the story had
changed.

It is human nature to sensationalize and exaggerate the facts.
In my opinion, this is why animals are so often credited with a

supernatural sixth sense; it makes for "good copy" or an interesting discussion. But it just is not true. Horses get "skittish" before an earthquake simply because they can feel and/or hear the sound waves before humans can. Dogs can detect cancer in people because of their superior sense of smell. There is nothing "supernatural" about these occurrences or the animals themselves.

I submit to you, however, that while animals do not have a supernatural sixth sense, *people do*. So you do not misunderstand me, I am not speaking of what we often refer to as the "paranormal." I am not referring to mediums or psychics, tarot card or palm readers, those who claim to be telekinetic or have ESP, illusionists, or anyone involved in anything like that. I am talking, rather, about everyday people, like you and me.

Generally speaking, people have an awareness of God and the supernatural. There is something inside each of us that "senses" the supernatural. It seems to be "standard factory issue" for humans. Granted, there is overwhelming diversity in what people actually believe, but the fact that they believe *something* seems to be a common denominator that distinguishes and perhaps even defines mankind. It is a peculiarity of humans, not seen in the animal kingdom.

And there are reasons this is true. In the book of **Romans, chapter 1**, we are told that humans know there is a God in one of three ways:

- 🐾 By our conscience (verse 19)
- 🐾 By the wonder of creation or nature (verse 20)
- 🐾 By the rest of the Word of God

There is no one, nor has there ever been anyone, who has not been exposed to at least one of these evidences of God's existence. Everyone has a conscience, or at least they did until they grew callous enough in their character to ignore it.

Moreover, everyone can perceive and appreciate the things that God has created, through the five senses He has given us. Even Helen Keller, after learning to master the disabilities of being unable to see or hear, spoke of the wonder of God's creation. She didn't have all of her senses, but those she did have were used to marvel at the wonder of God's handiwork.

Finally, almost everyone in the civilized world has at least heard of the Bible. Most have read at least a portion of it, or heard someone else refer to its authority and greatness.

God reveals Himself through our conscience, the wonder of His creation, and His Word.

If you travel the world as I have, you will see that every culture, every group of people, has a belief system in place. If you go to the darkest jungles of Africa or Asia, you will find natives bowing down before the head of a pig impaled on top of a spear, or worshiping an idol fashioned from raw materials from the forest. It seems that no matter how deeply you travel into the bush, or how primitive or godless the people you find there appear to be, you will always find some form of deity worship, some form of religion.

As I considered this, as I studied the Word of God, and as I recalled the literally thousands of conversations I have had with people about God throughout the years, a thought occurred to me. And that thought was this: that all people everywhere, in every time, in every culture, have something within them that tells them there is a God. It is something more than their conscience; it is a sixth sense, if you will.

They do not acquire this sense somewhere along the way in life. It is not taught in school (at least not anymore). It is just there, within them from birth. They may stray from the innocence of this realization later in their lives, depending upon their denominational affiliation or their personal experiences, but the sense that there is a God is inside all of us from the start. As I said before, it is not optional equipment, but standard factory issue for human beings, and I have never met a child without it.

It knows no race or gender. It is found on every continent, among every group of people. It is within each heart, placed there by the Creator, God. It doesn't matter if you are born in royalty or to a poor gaucho on a South American ranch. It doesn't matter if you are the child of a minister or if your parents are professed atheists. It is in you. It is a true sixth sense, if you will . . . not sight, not hearing, not taste, not smell, not touch, but something more.

It is not something that heightens the other senses, but another sense altogether—a sixth sense. It is something higher and greater, something that elevates our attention beyond the realm of our earthly existence. It gives us awareness that there is something more beyond our physical existence.

I call this sixth sense SONG, an acronym for **S**ense of **O**ur **N**eed for **G**od. Whether we realize it or not, inside each of us there exists a spiritual emptiness, or a yearning. We may have a successful and satisfying life. We may have amassed great wealth or achieved most or all of the goals we have set for ourselves. We may have attained fame or made a lasting contribution to society that gives us great personal satisfaction. Still, if we do not have a personal relationship with God, there remains a spiritual void, and our SONG has not yet been sung.

As an adult, you may not agree. Perhaps you have resisted, even ignored that aching, empty feeling. Maybe you have turned from God. Maybe you are an atheist yourself, or an agnostic. But I would wager you were not always so. I would imagine that as a child, you possessed the innocence that every child possesses, and you believed in God.

Let me repeat something I said earlier with stronger emphasis: I have ministered to thousands of children in my lifetime, and I have never met a child who did not believe in God. Children are inquisitive and ask a lot of difficult questions about God in order to understand Him better, but I have never had one tell me they did not believe in Him. There has not been time enough yet in their young lives for the world to have hardened their tender hearts or to have filled their innocent minds with religious error or humanism.

In fact, Jesus pointed to this innocence in **Matthew 19:14**, when He said to His disciples, "Suffer little children, and forbid them not, to come unto me; for of such is the kingdom of heaven." He was not saying that only children would be in heaven, but rather that those in heaven would have innocent faith and trust, like children have. And I think it is important to note that Jesus did not point out any specific children by name, but He generalized, indicating that all children possess this innocence and faith.

It has been my experience that Jesus' words ring true to this day. Children do not feel the spiritual emptiness that many adults feel. Perhaps it would be more accurate for me to say that adults no longer feel the innocence that they once felt as children. Innocence accepts that there is a God. Lack of innocence creates a void within. As our Creator, God knew this would be the case. So, driven by the love He has for us, God placed within each human heart that SONG, that we might recognize our need for Him and long after Him.

And that is why I was reluctant to include this question as part of this book. Children possess this SONG, and most of them believe in God without any hesitation. Therefore, it is unlikely that you will have this question posed to you by your child. More likely their questions will be framed with the presumption that God exists (i.e., "Where did God come from?" etc.). However, let us proceed under the presumption that some children may ask this question, and prepare an answer for them.

Hebrews 11 is commonly referred to as the "Hall of Faith." Here, more than a dozen well-known Bible characters are lauded for their faith in God. They are identified as champions and victors for their faith in God, not for any of the varied accomplishments we know them for from their Bible stories.

In **Hebrews 11:6**, we read these words:

> *But without faith it is impossible to please him;*
> *for he that cometh to God must believe that he is.*

Then, in **Ephesians 2:8** we also read:

For by grace are ye saved through faith.

Faith is what makes us right with God. It is His grace that reaches down to us and saves us, but we must exercise faith in order to receive that grace. **Hebrews 11:6** (above) says, "without faith . . ." We must have faith. It is the only way to please, or satisfy, God and to effect His grace.

So, what is faith? In the same verse, it tells us—we must "believe that God is." That is pretty straightforward: We must believe God *is*, or that He exists. The problem for many people is that they want to put the cart before the horse and have God prove that He exists before they will believe that He is. It doesn't work that way. That is not what God said. That is not the criteria He laid out.

But God is not unfair. As we learned before, He made sure that we all can know that He exists in many different ways. We each have that SONG within us. We each have a conscience. We each can see His handiwork in nature. And we have His Word. We have already discussed our sixth sense, so let us briefly analyze the other tools He has given us to help us generate our faith.

First up: our *conscience*. Webster defines the *conscience* as "an inner feeling or voice viewed as acting as a guide to the rightness or wrongness of one's behavior." I suppose that is an adequate definition, though I think "morals" and "ethics" should have been mentioned more directly. That notwithstanding, the conscience is proof of the existence of God. All goodness is ascribed to the person of God. When we use words like *holy*, *righteous*, *good*, *grace*, *mercy*, *love*, *benevolence*, etc., we associate them with God. Conversely, when we describe those who oppose God and all He stands for, the words we use are *evil*, *wicked*, *sinful*, *bad*, *dark*, etc.

Our conscience discerns the difference. Even the most ardent atheist will admit that when they struggle to do the right thing instead of ignoring their conscience and giving in to temptation, they congratulate themselves for doing right or good.

And *right* or *good* are terms we associate with God. Whether voluntarily or involuntarily, we have something built in to our conscience that gives God credit for good behavior. Or perhaps a better way to say it is that when we do good, we inwardly seek a sense of higher approval. However we articulate that feeling, I think it is safe to say that our conscience evidences the existence of God.

Next up: *nature*. Some can sear their conscience. By that, I mean they can become so callous and hard, so wicked, that they pay no attention to their conscience, if it even functions at all anymore. In this modern world of ours, we have all seen the utter depravity of men. That was not a mistake. I purposely said "men," because easily 99 percent of the horrific acts we witness around the globe are committed by men. And it is almost unfathomable how they can be so depraved and cause so much heartache and grief to others, seemingly without a twinge of remorse.

While I acknowledge that some can ignore their own conscience, they cannot ignore nature. There is no one who can avoid witnessing the wonder of the world around us. God's handiwork is everywhere. The universe is amazingly intricate and complex.

Let me camp out on this thought for a moment. Throughout the Bible, God heralds His creation to men and women. In the latter part of the book of Job and in other books of the Bible, He goes into minute detail about all He has created. He wants to be praised for His majesty and power. He wants us to marvel at His handiwork. Is it unreasonable that the God who made us and all that exists, who loves us and wants us to love Him, also wants to "wow" us with His creation? I don't think so.

I want to share a few scientifically verified facts about our universe that will simply astound you. In fact, they are so unbelievable that I guarantee you that, at least initially, you will think I made them up. But after checking me out on Google, you will know that I did not.

Science does not always get things right; evolution, the Big Bang, and global warming, to name a few of their miscues. But they have done an outstanding job at giving us a glimpse of the universe in which we live. Most people have no concept of what our extraordinary universe is comprised of.

It is inconceivably vast. The distance between some planets is billions of light-years. That is not a measurement of miles per se. It is a measurement of time. These planets are so far apart that it would take light, which travels at 156,000 miles per second, billions of years to travel between them. It takes light less than seven seconds to travel a million miles, but we are talking *billions of years*.

And some stars and planets are giants. Our own sun's mass

is more than a million times that of Earth's, but it is dwarfed by other gas giants like Arcturus, which itself is millions of times the size of our sun.

And the sheer number of other heavenly bodies is unfathomable. For decades, science has been using computerized telescopes to document and map planets and stars in our universe. Tools like Hubble and other telescopes in space have given them even greater abilities to accomplish this task.

Thus far, science has documented over one septillion stars, planets, and moons. Undoubtedly, this number means little to you. It is unlikely that you have ever seen the word used before. That is because it is such a huge number, there isn't a call for its use in everyday measurements.

One septillion is 10 to the 24th power. It is an incredibly long number that looks like this when written out: 1,000,000,000,000,000,000,000,000. That is how many planets today's scientists tell us are present in the known universe. And hold on to your hats: Science tells us that this is probably no more than 10 percent of what is out there.

The numbers break down like this. The universe is divided into four quadrants. Each quadrant is filled with galaxies. Within those galaxies there are solar systems, and within those solar systems there are planets, stars, and moons.

Our solar system, for instance, has nine planets (eight if you discount Pluto, as some do) and one star, our sun. Our solar system is in a galaxy known as the Milky Way. The Milky Way has nearly five hundred billion planets and stars in it. As extraordinary a number as this is, that is just one galaxy.

The Milky Way is one of approximately fifty billion galaxies in our quadrant, and each of the other quadrants contain a similar number of galaxies with a similar number of planets and stars in each. This gives us the overwhelming total of over one septillion. Let me try to illustrate this extraordinary number in terms that will better resonate with you.

One septillion is greater than all the words ever spoken by all the humans who have ever lived in the history of mankind. Before you balk at that figure, let me do the math for you. Get your calculator and follow along if you like.

The average person speaks between 3,000 and 8,000 words each day. That may not sound like much, but if you consider that a 45-minute speech usually uses about 4,000 words, you get a better idea of just how many words that is. On Sundays, when I teach, I use about 5,000 words, but on most other days, I use about 2,000. And I consider myself to be average.

But let us err in favor of doubt and say that the average is 10,000 words per day. That rules out any argument that the figures I have used are too conservative. I am essentially doubling what the average number of words spoken reasonably is.

Science estimates that 108 billion people have lived on Earth throughout our planet's history. I am not sure how they arrive at that figure, but we will assume it is correct, or at least in the ballpark.

The life expectancy of humans worldwide in modern times is approximately 56 years, but let's err again on the side of doubt and allow that it is 70 years. So the formula we would use is:

10,000 words per day × 365 days a year × 70
years × 108 billion people

This will result in a number that is followed by seventeen zeroes, far less than the twenty-four zeroes in a septillion. This would mean that the number of planets in the universe is ten million times greater than the number of words ever spoken thus far on this planet.

I warned you that the numbers I was going to share with you would be difficult to believe. Even now you are probably sure that I made a mistake in my math. I understand, because I had to check and recheck the facts and figures several times. But I assure you that they are correct.

Now then, if you think that illustration was extraordinary, try wrapping your mind around this next one: One septillion is more than the number of leaves on every tree on every continent on Planet Earth.

Now, unless you are a recluse or bedridden, you have taken drives out in the country and seen a lot of trees. In most parts of the world, you don't have to go very far to find thick forests covering the landscape, with so many trees it seems you could never count them all, let alone the leaves that are on them.

Now, let me quantify this illustration for you. By *trees*, I mean *every type* of mature tree, including all in the deciduous and coniferous family groups (which includes all evergreens).

And by *leaves*, I mean every type of leaf and pine needle. Science estimates that the average adult tree has between 50,000 and 150,000 leaves or pine needles. Again, erring to doubt's favor, let's use 200,000 as our base number.

NASA has evaluated their photographic portfolio of Earth and estimated that there are approximately four hundred billion adult trees on Earth. This includes the rain forests and the taiga or bo-real forests of the north.

If you are unfamiliar with the taiga, it is a swath of trees from 300 to 1,000 miles wide that loops around the northern part of our globe. Part of it extends as far south as Minnesota and Wisconsin, but most of it is found in the northern countries of Canada, Russia, China, and so on. NASA's estimate does not include saplings and bushes, only adult trees.

With so many trees, it seems you could never count them all.

Using their figures, along with science's estimate of the average number of leaves on a tree, the resulting number comes out to a figure with only eighteen zeroes following it. Again, this number falls far short of a septillion, and it would take all the leaves on all the trees on a million Earths to equal the number of planets that science has documented in our universe. And that is just 10 percent of what science says is out there!

The question could be asked, Why did God make the universe so huge, with so many planets and stars? The only possible answer is that God doesn't do things in a small way. He desires to be worshiped and praised by His creation, and that would be an unreasonable expectation if He did not display His great power and ability.

The point I want to make about all of this is that with all these planets and stars that God has made, as far as we know, Earth is the only planet with life on it. Astronomers have closely scrutinized millions upon millions of other celestial bodies and have found no signs of life on them. Only Earth has life.

Our Earth is the perfect size, generating the optimal gravitational pull to allow us to be mobile. It is the perfect size to accommodate the humans that God created, in the perfect position to benefit from the sun's light and gravitational pull, and perfect in a thousand other ways.

Our moon is perfectly placed to create tides, and more importantly, to generate more than fifty ocean currents that keep the seas from becoming stagnant. The currents also transfer heat from landmasses and dissipate it into the sea, instigating the process of evaporation so that storms develop to bring water back to the land. Admittedly, that is an oversimplification, but I don't think I need to explain to you the process of evaporation in much detail.

Everything on Earth—and in the universe—works as if a Master Designer had put it together. And, indeed, one did. But the beauty and wonder of nature, and the way everything works together so perfectly, should promote, even provoke faith in God. How can anyone deny the facts that they can see with their own eyes?

Finally: the *Word of God.* More than our conscience and the wonder of nature, the Word of the living God, the Bible, convinces us of the reality and existence of God. The Bible is not a book; it is the will and words of God transferred to paper through holy men so we might have them and live by them. The Bible alone is the authority of God in this world. In **Hebrews 4:12** we are told:

> *For the word of God is quick [alive], and power-*
> *ful, and sharper than any two-edged sword, pierc-*
> *ing even to the dividing asunder of soul and spirit,*
> *and of the joints and marrow, and is a discerner*
> *of the thoughts and intents of the heart.*

No other book is alive or can accomplish the things that the Bible accomplishes in the hearts of men and women. No other book can discern or perceive the thoughts and intents of people. Only God's Word has that power and authority.

The Bible has been the best-selling book in history. Yes, it has even outsold popular fantasy books about wizards and other imaginary characters. The Bible, unlike fantasy novels, does not provide escape from reality, but forces us to face it: to see the truth and our need for reconciliation with God.

No other book has changed millions of lives, sobered up drunkards, changed the hearts of thieves and harlots, or brought peace to even one soul; this blessed, powerful book has. Men have tried to destroy it. Others have tried to disprove it by bringing railing, false accusations against it. Still others have tried to expose it as a book of lies written by men, as was once the folly of this author, but instead, they were themselves exposed as liars (again, this author included).

A wise old preacher once responded to the accusations that the Bible was written by men by saying, "How can that be; for if wicked men wrote it, they have condemned themselves. If good men wrote it, they too have condemned themselves for the Bible says 'For all have sinned and come short of the glory of God.' That only leaves us with the one who claimed to write it, God."

We could treat the matter as one would a case in a court of law. We can find from a preponderance of the evidence for, and a lack of evidence against, the proposition that God, indeed, truly exists. However, God does not want men to weigh the evidence in a legalistic way, but rather in their hearts. He desires faith to be the outcome of His revelation of Himself through our conscience, through nature, and through His Word.

What to Share with Your Child
QUESTION: *"Is God real, Mommy?"*

As I mentioned earlier, I have my doubts about this being a question that children commonly ask, but we need to be prepared in case they do. Of all questions we will address, this is probably the one that parents (as adults) can appreciate the most.

Is there one among us who has not questioned the existence of God? Even within the hearts of the strongest in faith among us, occasionally doubts can creep in. Oh, we are reluctant to admit it, but it is true.

For many adults who find themselves doubting, or whose faith has suffered a setback and is weak, it can require much work and great effort to get back to that place of faith where we feel secure. But that is not the case for children; their innocence makes them accepting and trusting. You might find the following matrix very helpful should your child need his or her faith reinforced.

I am so glad you told me that this was bothering you. It is good for us to talk about important things like this. Everyone should know about God, and it is important that we are able to tell them why we know He is real.

One of the ways we know that God is real is because He wrote a book to tell us that He is, and that book is the Bible. You know that we look at the Bible each evening as a family and we talk about the wonderful things that God did for people just like you and me who lived a long time ago. We read about the miracles God did and how He did them to help people and to show them that He loved them.

Now, there are other books that talk about people who do magic and sorcery, or who are superheroes, but those are just make-believe stories. Those characters are not real, and there is no one who can really do those things. People write books and make movies like that, because people like to read and watch fantasy.

But the Bible is real, and so is the God whom we read about in it. You know what history is, right? It is when people who were alive long ago wrote about what happened and left those writings for us to read. Like when Christopher Columbus discovered the Americas . . . he wrote official records that we have today telling us about it. Or when America became a country, we have papers that men signed to show how we declared ourselves to be free.

That is what the Bible is: a record that God made for us to read many years later so we would know about Him and believe in Him. But God knew that because He is in another place and we can't see Him right now, just reading about Him wouldn't be enough for us to believe. So He did some other things to help us believe.

The first thing He did was to give us a conscience. Do you know what your conscience is? Do you remember when you were throwing your ball in the house and broke the lamp and then told me that it was the dog that did it? That was not the truth, but I wanted to believe you, so I did. But then later that day, you came to me and said you weren't telling me the truth and that you felt really bad about lying to me.

Well, that was your conscience working. Our conscience tells us what is right and wrong. People sometimes want to do things that are wrong, but God wants us to do things that are right. When we do right, we feel good. But when we do wrong, we feel bad. Our conscience is God's way of helping us to do right and feel good about it. So when our conscience helps us to do good, we see that God is helping us to want that. And we know that He is real.

Another way we know that God is real is by looking around at all that He has made. Our world is beautiful. There is no other place like Earth. Do you know how many planets God made? There are more planets in outer space than there are leaves on all the trees you have ever seen. That's a lot, isn't it? Now, we can't go to all those planets, but we have been able to look at them through big, powerful telescopes, and not one of those other planets look anything like Earth.

There are no oceans, no lakes, no trees, no flowers, no animals, and no people. Only our planet has all those things—and more. We have a sun to give us light and to warm us. It helps vegetables to grow. And I know you don't like vegetables that much, but they are good for us. And the sun also helps fruit to grow. We have rivers and lakes and clean water to drink. We have air to breathe and animals everywhere.

All of these things are here because God made them. And He made them for us so that we would believe in Him and in His love for us. One day we will see Him, when we go to be where He is. And then we will know that our belief, or faith, in Him was right. And we will be happy to be with Him and to enjoy all that He has for us in heaven.

And not only does He love people, but He loves the animals He created, too. And all of them will get to see Him one day, too. Our Buddy is there with Him right now, and isn't it good to know that he is happy there?

God is most certainly real. Sometimes we wonder about that. It is hard sometimes to believe, because we cannot see Him. But we cannot see the wind, but we still know it is there. We cannot see love, but we still feel it for each other. And so we can't see God until we go to be with Him someday, but we know that He is there. We can feel Him in our hearts, and we can see Him in the wonder and beauty of the things He has made.

Chapter 3

"Why Did God Let Buddy Die?"

This simple question from a grieving child is an innocent expression of the way they feel. They perceive God as all-powerful, which He is, and because of that they expect that He has control over everything that happens in our world. It is only natural for them to wonder why God allows bad things to happen. The assumption is erroneous, of course, but a reasonable one from an innocent child's point of view.

Unfortunately, this erroneous assumption is shared by most adults, too, Christians and non-Christians alike. The difference between a child and an adult is profound, however. A child's question is more wondering out loud than accusatory. When an adult asks, "Why did God . . ." it is generally to affix blame where they think it belongs.

The fact is that, except for when God punishes evil, God does not visit bad things upon people. He is not even tempted to. His will toward men, women, and children is always positive. In **James 1:17** we are told that "every good gift [that means all of them] and every perfect gift is from above. . . ." Good things come from God. He rejoices when He is able to shower us with goodness and good things.

Just a couple of verses earlier, in **James 1:15**, he tells us that the bad things that befall us in this world, up to and including death, come from sin, not from God. If we suffer in this world, it is the result of sin, the one thing in all creation that God hates.

God knew what impact sin would have upon us, how it would corrupt the world, which, in turn, would cause bad things to befall us. That is why He tried to protect Adam and Eve from temptation in the Garden of Eden. He knew that as soon as they sinned, the perfect world He had created for them, where bad things never happened, would change.

That is why, years later, He gave us laws and rules to live by, to offset or reduce the impact of this sinful world upon us. The Ten Commandments are a good example of this. Some accuse God of being a bully by giving us these commandments, dictating to us how we should live our lives and limiting our choices and free will.

My goodness, nothing could be further from the truth. The Ten Commandments were given by God from a position of love to help us, to make our lives better. Knowing human nature and our propensity to sin, He gave these commandments, and other social tenets and laws, to keep us from doing things that would harm us emotionally and spiritually.

When He said, "Thou shalt not bear false witness" (Exodus 20:16), He was trying to keep us from doing something that would lead to the degrading and numbing of our conscience and moral bearing. He knew that even the smallest lie would have an adverse effect on our character, making it easier for us to lie again and again and again.

When He admonished us to "honor thy father and thy mother . . ." it was to establish good family and social orders, because without that we would have anarchy or worse. And so, all the commandments and laws were given, not because God wanted to flex His muscle over us, but because He wanted nothing but good things to happen in our lives. By adhering to these principles and guidelines, we would save ourselves and those we love from much heartache and trouble.

The counterargument to this is that God has providential will, and if He wants something to happen, or not to happen, all He has to do is invoke it. Therefore, if something bad happens, it is because God allowed it to happen. So indirectly, He is to blame.

The first two points are true. God does have absolute authority and providential will. And the fact that He does not stop something bad from happening does technically mean that He allowed it to happen. But I used the word *technically* here purposefully. This topic is much more complicated than it first appears to be.

God has two wills: His *providential* will and His *permissive* will. His providential will is absolute and there is no variance allowed. A few examples of this absolute will include:

- 🐾 Salvation is only attainable through the atonement of His Son, Jesus Christ. There is no other way. In the book of John, it is recorded that Jesus said, "I am the way, the truth, and the life: no man cometh unto the Father, but by me" (14:6).

🐾 The Bible is His Word, and there is no other authority.

🐾 Believers should be members of local assemblies.

There are many things we could add to this list, but I think most readers understand the types of things that are providentially set in granite by God. What we really are concerned about is God's permissive will; in which He allows things to happen or to come to pass—or not.

Now, this word *permissive* is used advisedly. It confers the false idea that God somehow signs off on a thing and then it happens. Not so. It simply is a term that acknowledges that God is omniscient, and therefore He knows when a thing will happen—but that does not mean that He approves of it or even wants it to happen.

God has given us free will. His extension of this right to us is not fickle. He doesn't allow us to decide some things and not other things. He gives us absolute free will. For instance, He desires that we join a local church and worship Him, but if we choose not to do so, He doesn't force us to. He allows us to disobey His will and to follow our own. That is free will.

The ramifications for His allowing us this right are obvious. We are going to create problems in our lives, and others who exercise their free will are going to create other problems for us. If someone you do not know is speeding down the highway recklessly and slams into your vehicle, that isn't God's will. It wasn't even your will. It was a product of another person's will and actions.

We can hardly blame God for something like that. Yes, He knew about it before it happened, but in order for Him to intervene, He would have had to rescind the right of free will for that person speeding in the car. Or perhaps He could have rescinded our free will by having us involuntarily turn our vehicle before we arrived at the point of impact.

But then, of course, this arbitrary and constant giving and rescinding of people's free will would, in effect, result in there not being free will at all. If God could arbitrarily interject His will over ours, then everything that happened in our lives would be dependent upon His will and not ours. And then truly we could assign blame to Him for all of the bad things that happened.

But that is not the way things are. That is not what God wants. Clearly, in His Word, He tells us that He extends this right to us, so that we can make our own decisions. He gives us free will in everything, so that we might choose to know Him. He wants us to willingly place our faith and trust in Him and live our lives according to His will, but by our own free choice.

Could He force us to believe? Of course He could. But He doesn't want mindless drones, but rather, willing hearts to love and serve Him.

To automatically blame God for the bad things that befall us is wrong and unjust. God wants us only to have good things. He is the Source of all good. Even when bad things come into our lives, He proactively brings good from that bad. And instead of falsely accusing Him of bringing the bad, we ought to adore Him and praise Him for the good He visits upon us.

Matthew Henry, the great Welsh Bible historian and commentator of the seventeenth century, was once mugged and robbed on the street. When asked if he blamed God for this awful thing that had befallen him, he responded, "No, I am thankful to God. I am thankful that I had something worthy of being robbed; I am thankful that while the robber took my purse he did not take my life; I am thankful that while he took all that I had, it was not very much; and finally, I am thankful that it was I who was robbed and not I who robbed."

Oh, to have our faith in proper order as this man had. His faith found no reason to blame God for his misfortune, but many ways to give thanks in spite of it.

When a child asks a question like, "Mommy, why did God allow Buddy to die?" or "Why didn't God let Buddy live longer?" our answer must have more content than, "Well, we can't know why God does things. We just have to trust that He knows what He is doing." Answers like this serve only to confirm to the child that God somehow had something to do with the bad thing that happened, and that just is not true.

Children need to know that bad things happen to everyone. They even happened to Jesus and His disciples. Bad things happen in this world because it is a bad place with many bad people in it. God is not one of them. God is good, and God does only good things.

Yes, a bad thing happened to Buddy and to your family. But talk with your children about all the good things that God did in relation to Buddy and your family. For instance, you might offer that:

- God brought us Buddy because He knew Buddy needed people to love him.
- God brought us Buddy because He knew we needed Buddy's love.

🐾 God gave Buddy a long life with us.

🐾 God made Buddy's life happy.

🐾 God made a place for Buddy in heaven for when he got old.

🐾 God helped this family to help each other when we were sad.

🐾 God tells us that we will see Buddy again.

Perspective gives birth to outlook and attitude. If children are allowed to believe that somehow God is behind their pain, it will adversely change their perspective of God and undoubtedly their attitude toward Him. If they are shown that God is the Benefactor of all the good in their lives, and none of the bad, that perspective will be one of thanks, and the resulting attitude will be upbeat and positive toward God. If this world had more people who truly knew God for who He is, there would be far fewer people perpetrating bad acts against the rest of us.

What to Share with Your Child
QUESTION: *"Why did God let Buddy die?"*

When you ask that question, it makes me think that you feel that God made Buddy die. I hope you know that God didn't do that. God only wants good things for His animals, just like He wants good things for people and angels.

Our Buddy died because he got old and his body just didn't work well anymore. It wasn't God's fault. It wasn't Buddy's fault, either. It is just how things work in this world. Living things get old and die.

But it wasn't supposed to be that way in the beginning. When God made the world, He made it perfect. Adam and Eve were not meant to grow old. The animals in the Garden with them were not meant to get old. Even the flowers weren't meant to get old and die like they do today. And no one ever got sick.

That was the way God wanted it to be for all of us. But we all know the story of how Adam and Eve sinned by disobeying God. And as soon as they did, it ruined all of what God had made.

Adam and Eve started to get older, and so did all of the animals. The flowers and trees started to get older, and bad things started to happen. Some of the trees grew thorns, and some of the insects started to bite and sting.

And now we have a world where a lot of bad things happen all the time.

- 🐾 Animals die.
- 🐾 People die.
- 🐾 People and animals get sick.
- 🐾 There is crime.
- 🐾 Some people go hungry.

These are all things that God did not want for our world. But do you know why God doesn't stop them from happening? It is because He has given us something called free will. All that means is that God loves us so much that He allows us to make our own choices. And when people make bad choices, sometimes bad things happen.

Remember when you thought that you were strong enough to hold Buddy on his leash and how he pulled you off your feet when he ran after that squirrel? You fell down and skinned your knee. You made a bad choice, and something bad happened.

Well, God lets all people make their own choices. He doesn't want us to be mindless robots, like we see on television. (Imitate a robot talking to the kids and making robot moves.) "Yes, master; no, master."

God allows us to think about and do things our own way. He lets the whole world run all by itself automatically.

- 🐾 The sun comes up each day.
- 🐾 The sun sets each evening.
- 🐾 The rain waters the plants.
- 🐾 The flowers grow.
- 🐾 And life goes on each day.

Part of life is that people and animals get old and die. Buddy died because he got old. God did not make him get old. It is just what happens in this world since it changed when Adam and Eve sinned.

So, God is not to blame for Buddy dying. God doesn't do bad things. He does only good. Think about all the good things He did for us with Buddy.

- 🐾 God brought us Buddy because He knew Buddy needed people to love him.
- 🐾 God brought us Buddy because He knew we needed Buddy's love.
- 🐾 God gave Buddy a long life with us.
- 🐾 God made Buddy's life happy.

🐾 *God made a place for Buddy in heaven for when he got old.*

🐾 *God helped this family to help each other when we were sad.*

🐾 *God will let us see Buddy again one day.*

We ought to thank God for all of these good things He does for us to make us feel better about the bad things that the world gives us. Would you like to thank God with me right now as a family? I will pray out loud for all of us and thank Him.

Chapter 4

"Does God Love Buddy?"

The simple answer, of course, is "yes." Ordinarily, a simple answer would satisfy a child. But given the circumstances of having just lost their best friend, it is almost certain that your child is looking for a longer and more detailed response. My guess is that if your children ask you this question, they will do so with an unusually serious tone and an expectancy uncommon to someone of their age level.

Undoubtedly, like all young children, they have already (or will) bombard you with the normal wide variety of questions that youngsters commonly ask. They are usually nothing more than mundane inquiries, such as, "Why do we call birds, birds?" or "How does a water fountain work?" etc.

Some of their questions might even make you wonder whether their thinking process is working properly. My son, for instance, once asked me, "Dad, do you think I can sit still for one hour without moving or blinking?" Of course, I knew he couldn't, but at the moment I had some things that I needed to take care of, so I knew that I had to choose my words carefully or be stuck observing his attempt to achieve this lofty goal.

45

So I decided to fib a little and say, "Why, yes, I do," in hopes that my response would register as a triumph to him, he would walk away beaming, and the matter would then be closed. It didn't, he didn't, and it wasn't. Instead, he quickly snapped back with, "Oh, great! Okay, watch," and before I could find another way to wiggle out of the situation, he went into a frozen, robot-like pose.

As I inwardly expected, he lasted no more than eight seconds—then he blinked, chuckled at his failure, and said, "Okay, wait, wait, I can do it." He tried again. He didn't succeed. After perhaps a half-dozen more tries, he still hadn't succeeded. So he quit. I had actually started enjoying the entertainment, but was happy he hadn't been able to do it and thus keep me there for the full hour.

When children ask adults questions like this, sometimes they are being inquisitive and want to know an answer, but usually they just like talking and the questions are more rhetorical than anything else. At worst, usually a "yes" or "no" will suffice for an answer, and they will go back to whatever it was they were doing.

Now, I am not suggesting we should avoid our children's questions or that they are not important. Rather, I am trying to show the difference between everyday inquisitive comments and the concerns expressed by a grieving child. When a serious question is asked during a time of bereavement, if at all possible, parents need to stop what they are doing, give their child their full attention, and focus on the question being asked.

It also will be of great help if you are prepared with answers that will satisfy them. That is why this guide was organized and made available for parents: to ensure that you do not get caught by surprise and have to delay or defer an answer when your child needs one.

Regarding the title question for this chapter, fortunately, there is no shortage of passages in the Scriptures that point to God's love for His animals. The fact that our pets belong to God is an extremely important concept to get across to your children. They should know that He entrusted us with their care because He knew we would love them and care for them. But they are His animals as much as we are His people.

God loves all that He has created. . . .

It has been my experience that when you share this knowledge with a child, they connect all the dots in their mind and begin to carry on an internal conversation with themselves to reconcile these new thoughts . . .

🐾 *Buddy really belongs to God . . .*
🐾 *I belong to God . . .*
🐾 *And God loves me . . .*
🐾 *So He must love Buddy, too.*

That may seem overly simplistic to you, but I assure you, I have seen this process work in children over and over again. They mull over this new prospect that their pet really belongs to God, and before long they like that idea. Their tender little hearts find peace in knowing that God has a personal interest in them and their pets. It is as if, all of a sudden, God is sharing their pain with them, because God loves their pet as much as they do.

But let's get to some of the passages that help us to understand how God feels about His animals. In the very first chapter of the Bible, **Genesis 1**, we have the record that God created the animals. He also created everything else, including mankind, but for now let's keep our focus on the animals.

In **Genesis 1:31**, God assesses all that He had created. And what was His assessment? Did He say, "Now, why did I make those pesky, smelly skunks?" or "Yuck, what was I thinking when I made snakes and jellyfish?" No, of course He didn't. He said something very profound and powerful, recorded proof of how He feels about His creatures. This verse says:

> *And God saw every thing that he had made,*
> *and, behold, it was very good.*

Now, I could be wrong, but I think this was as much a resounding positive review of His love for the animals He had created, as it was for His own ability to create. He did not say that they were merely good, but "very" good. He was quite pleased.

And this providential care and concern for animals is seen throughout the Scriptures. Ordinarily, I would say that this preponderance of evidence proves that God loves His animals. But I don't think we need collective proof, because each of the accounts I am going to list below is stand-alone proof of His love. Let's take a quick glimpse at some of the important moments between God and animals in the Bible.

- ❧ *The Garden of Eden:* God united mankind and animalkind in mutual companionship. Animals were tame, without prey or predator. God made them all vegetarians and provided for their care. They were important to His plan.
- ❧ *The Ark:* Of course, God was going to save Noah and the other seven members of his family, but He had Noah spend one hundred years building the ark to carry His creatures to safety and to ensure their continuance on the earth. They remained important to His plan.
- ❧ *The Manger:* Was it by chance that there was no room in the inn on the night when Jesus the Lord was born? Jesus was born in a stable among His innocent creatures. Joseph and Mary were there, but then, they had to be there. The shepherds were not present until they were summoned later that night, and the Magi did not arrive for approximately two years. But the animals remained important.
- ❧ *Jesus' Time of Fasting:* The forty days of fasting that Jesus performed in the wilderness was not in the company of His disciples or His family members, but "with the wild

beasts." Once again, it was the animals that were in the spotlight.

-   *The Millennium:* During the final thousand-year millennium, animals will be reinstated to the status they enjoyed in the Garden of Eden, companions to mankind, with no prey or predator.
-   *God's Word:* When you add to this God's repeated instructions throughout the Scriptures on how to kindly treat and care for animals, His revelation that He clothes the sparrow, cares for the fox, and tells herds when to migrate north and south, God's loving, watchful care over His creatures becomes as obvious as their importance to Him.

God has shown consistent interest in and care over the animals He created. He has provided guidance on how to treat the animals, and He has told us that they are eternal essences or personalities. But is there more that we can say about His love that would help our children trust that He loves their pets? I believe there is.

In **1 John 4:8**, we are told:

> *He that loveth not, knoweth not God,*
> *for God is love.*

Here is one of the most important and potent verses in the Bible. This verse does not say that God loves, though we know He does. It also does not say that He can love. It says that He *is* love. It is His very nature. Love does not exist without God. And since God is also immutable, which means that He cannot change, then His nature is to love constantly and eternally.

God loves all that He has created. He hates only sin, but then, He did not create sin. Satan did. But let me shock you, and this might really shock you. God is love. He loves all that He created. And He loves all that He created without end. So here comes the shock: That means that He still loves Satan and all his demons.

Yes, you heard me right. God loves Satan and his horde of demons. Of course, He hates their sin and He deplores the evil they have done, but He is immutable. He loves them eternally. He cannot help but love them, because His nature is love. And because of that everlasting love, He will never utterly destroy them. They will suffer punishment under His wrath, but we are told that they will never be annihilated.

If He still loves these wicked creatures, how can anyone doubt that He loves His other loving, devoted, and innocent creatures? How can anyone even suggest that God would allow them simply to cease to exist?

Does God love His animals? Does God love Buddy? Without a doubt, He does.

What to Share with Your Child

QUESTION: *"Does God love Buddy?"*

I know this is a very important question to you. You ask me a lot of questions every day, but this one is special to you, I know.

You and I love a lot of things, don't we? We love them because they belong to us and we want to take care of them. Some of the things we might own and love are:

- 🐾 *Our pets*
- 🐾 *Our toys*
- 🐾 *Our clothes*
- 🐾 *Our books*

You see what I mean? We love our pets, and we want to take care of them. We love our toys and books, and we want to make sure we take care of them and don't break them. We wash our clothes so they aren't dirty because we care about them.

God is a lot like us. He has things that belong to Him that He loves. Our earth is one of them. God made this earth. He made all of the beautiful forests and trees. He made the beautiful blue lakes and oceans. He made the majestic mountains and the green valleys. And He owns all of them. He loves it all, and He wants to take care of it.

But you know what? God also owned Buddy. That's right. Buddy belonged to God. He always belonged to God. God let him stay with us, because He knew that you would love Him, too, and that you would take very good care of him. And you did.

God owns all the animals. And he loves them and takes care of them. When they get too sick or old to stay here on the earth anymore, He takes them home to be with Him in heaven. He never stops loving them. That is how I know He loves Buddy.

But there is more. Did you know that all through the Bible, there are stories of how God takes care of His animals? Let me tell you about a few of them.

- 🐾 *First, there was the Garden of Eden. I don't know how big the Garden was, but all the animals that God made lived in the Garden with Adam and Eve. There were tigers and bears, and lions and elephants. But all of those animals were tame. They were like pets for Adam and Eve. God loved the animals so much that He gave them a beautiful garden to live in without any danger.*
- 🐾 *Then there was the ark. When God decided to destroy the earth because people had become so evil, He spared Noah and his family, but He also saved the animals. He loved them. He had Noah build a big enough boat, the ark, to carry them all through the flood. Did you know it took Noah a hundred years to build the ark? But God wanted His animals to be safe.*
- 🐾 *Next, there was the manger. When Jesus was born, His mother was there and so was Joseph. But there were no other people, only animals. Jesus was the only completely innocent baby ever born, and I guess God wanted Him to be born among the innocent animals that He loved.*
- 🐾 *Then there was a time when Jesus didn't eat for forty days. Can you imagine not eating for forty days? Wow. But during that time, He didn't stay around His family or friends. Instead, the Bible tells us that He went out into the wilderness and stayed with the wild animals. I am sure they knew who He was. They knew that He loved them.*

🐾 *Finally, did you know that when Jesus comes back to earth again, all the animals are going to be tame again? That's right—children will walk with lions like they do with their dogs today. God will make all the animals tame again, because He loves them and He wants us to love them, too.*

Never worry about God loving Buddy. He certainly does, and He always will. And Buddy knows it, I am sure. But don't ever forget that God loves us, too, and one day He will bring us all together again.

Chapter 5

"WHERE IS BUDDY RIGHT NOW?"

I nevitably, you are going to be asked this question in one form or another by your child. Where their best friend has gone is almost the first thought a child has after losing a cherished pet. And it is as important as any question they will ask.

I would strongly suggest that you try to avoid worn-out platitudes such as, "Well, Buddy is in a better place," or "Buddy is right here in our hearts with us." Those types of answers come across as condescending and disingenuous.

And even though your child may not know what either of those two words—*condescending* or *disingenuous*—mean, they certainly know when you are talking down to them or are just saying whatever comes to mind so you do not have to explain something difficult to them.

Don't use platitudes or halfhearted answers. Children can usually see right through them, and if they do, you will lose credibility with your children. An honest and direct approach is undoubtedly the better way to go.

If you are able, offer more than what they asked about (i.e., "Buddy is in heaven at this very moment, kids. Would you like me to tell you a little about what heaven is like?" etc.). Offering more will show them that you are listening and that you are genuinely concerned about how they feel.

You can get by with just the first half of such a response, but you can expect that leaving it there will just lead to other questions anyway, at least for most children. Telling children that a pet is in heaven is helpful and direct, but it usually is not enough. That answer will probably lead them to the next logical question: "But how can Buddy be in heaven if his body is in the ground where we buried him yesterday?"

Well, there is a "gotcha" moment if there ever was one. I don't care what the so-called child behavior experts say, you can never be sure about what a child is going to think of or say next. The fact that we were once children ourselves does not give us an edge in that department, either. We have long left our "anything is possible" childhood cognitive processes behind. As adults, most of us think in regimental paradigms.

When we think we know what a child is thinking, and especially when we think that we are sure, that is when they prove just how little we truly know. Kids have a propensity for catching adults off guard and disarming them.

In the 1960s, the late comedian Art Linkletter hosted a weekly television show called *Kids Say the Darndest Things*. So you aren't confused, this was the original series. Later the show was brought back with Bill Cosby as the host.

In the original series, each week Mr. Linkletter would bring several children, ages approximately five through twelve, up on the stage after they were randomly picked from the audience. He would spend a few minutes with each child talking and interviewing them.

If memory serves me correctly, I think that was the format for the entire show. I don't recall it ever being a variety show or having guest celebrities do cameos. But that format was entertaining enough. Mr. Linkletter appeared to use no script. He would simply ask general questions of the children, such as:

- What is your name?
- How old are you?
- Where are you from?

After he felt the children were comfortable enough talking with him in front of the camera, he would then ask them more probing questions, obviously hoping to evoke a response that the audiences there and at home would find humorous. Some of the questions were purposely silly, while others were legitimate inquiries. But the hope was that the child would say something worthy of humor. Here are several examples:

- Are you married?
- Who is your best friend?
- Do you have an older sister?
- What is her boyfriend's name?
- Is he cute?
- What does your daddy do?

Invariably, at least one of the children he interviewed would innocently let slip some personal family secret that would have the audience in stitches. You can Google the show and find several videos of such moments if you like. One that I distinctly remember, but could not find a clip on, was when Mr. Linkletter spoke with a little girl from New York City. After the normal welcoming questions, the conversation went something like this:

LINKLETTER: So, tell me, honey, what does your daddy do?

GIRL: Oh, my daddy fought in the war.

LINKLETTER: So, your daddy was a soldier in Korea or somewhere else?

GIRL: Oh no, he fought with the police when they came to our house.

The studio audience was briefly stunned by the young girl's answer. A hushed silence came over them, but a few moments later they erupted into laughter.

The parents, who were in the audience, were undoubtedly mortified by the answer and the fear that the host might pursue more information. But Mr. Linkletter was both a gentleman and a gentle man and went no further.

This is a showcase example that proves that we can never be sure of what is going on in a child's mind. Their responses to our questions can surprise us, but more importantly, the questions they themselves ask can catch us off guard.

Mr. Linkletter accumulated scores of surprise responses over the years. I think he would strongly agree that you might think you know what kids are going to say, but the truth is, kids do say the darndest things.

Having your child ask how Buddy can be in heaven when his body is in the ground is a good example of this truth. We adults readily accept and embrace this concept, and it would not occur to us that somehow the two truths conflict with each other. But in a child's mind it may, and this could be a huge stumbling block for children while dealing with their grief and sorrow.

To answer the question, "Where is Buddy right now?" satisfactorily for your child, I would like to take you back to a Bible verse that we used earlier. In **Job 12:10** it says:

In whose hand is the soul of every living thing. . . .

I think it would help to explain to children what the word *soul* means in this portion of the Scriptures. Doing so will allow you

"In whose hand is the soul of every living thing . . ." (Job 12:10)

to present them with an illustration that should help them understand how a physical body and one's soul can be in two different places. Or, how it applies to their question, how Buddy's body can be in the ground and his soul can also be in heaven.

To remind you, the word *soul* in this verse is the Hebrew word *nephesh*, and it means "one's essence," or "life force." Now, that may sound a little like Zen philosophy (i.e., "total togetherness of mind and body," etc.), but it is not meant to sound that way.

All that the word *essence* means is "what we are" or "who we are." The official definition is: "a property or group of properties of something without which it would not exist or be what it is." That is just too stuffy and complex for me, though I prefer to just say that our essence is who we are. Makes more sense, doesn't it?

So, what does all this mean in terms of answering our question? Simply, it means that we are not a body with a soul, but a soul with a body. The difference may seem subtle, but it is not. It is huge. Our body is the house in which our soul lives, and when the body dies, our soul leaves that house and continues to live on. God has determined that when this happens, the souls of people will leave this world and go to the next.

Our soul is our essence, not our body. The soul is who we are, not the body. Our soul, or essence, consists of our:

- 🐾 Consciousness
- 🐾 Personality

- Cognitive functions
- Emotions
- Memories
- Religious beliefs
- Ethics and morals

That is not a complete list, but it is enough for you to get the idea. When a person or an animal dies, we look at their body and miss the life that was in that body. That life is the soul, and it has been relocated by God. We pay honor to the body by burying it and marking where it lies with nice epitaphs and flowers, and so on. But it is the soul of the person or the animal that we truly miss.

You might try to give your children an illustration to help them understand the separating of the soul from the body. You might come up with a better one, but here are a few that you might consider using:

- A hermit crab leaves its shell behind in order to move to another, better shell. So, too, the soul leaves its earthly body and relocates to a better body in heaven.

At this point, children do not have to understand that souls are given a better, temporary body in heaven, pending the resurrection and glorification of the old one. So, unless they ask, don't explain all of that to them at this time. That would only confuse them. Keep your answers true, but keep them as simple as possible so they can understand.

☺ A caterpillar enters into a cocoon, from which it immediately leaves its body and flies away as a glorious butterfly. We leave our earthly bodies behind, and our glorified souls fly away.

It should now be an easy step to explain to your child how Buddy's body, or shell, was left behind and his soul, or essence, went to heaven, just like people do. Make a mental note to explain the "temporary body" issue to them at a later, more appropriate time. The chances are that, as they mull over all that you have taught them through this experience, they will later figure out that there is another body involved in this process and ask you about it anyway.

But this should be enough information at this point for you to answer their question.

What to Share with Your Child

QUESTION: *"Where is Buddy right now?"*

You want to know where Buddy is right now. As usual, that is a very good question. And the best way for me to answer your question is to ask you a question of my own. And this is it: Do you know what a soul is?

Give your children time to think about the question and answer it. If they don't know the answer, that is okay; don't push them. But if they try to answer it, let them finish, acknowledge and praise their responses, and then continue.

Those were great answers, kids. Thank you. But can I add some-thing to what you said? We know that God is one God and that He is the only God. But do you remember learning in Sunday school that God is actually three persons in one—God the Father, Jesus the Son, and the Holy Spirit? That is called "triune." God is a triune Being.

Well, when God made us, he made us the same way, as triune beings. We have:

- *A body*
- *A soul*
- *And a spirit*

We are made in three parts, just like God is three parts or per-sons. But I am only going to talk about two of those parts, the body and the soul, right now so that I can answer your question about where Buddy is right now.

When we die, our body stops working, and there is no more life in it. We honor someone's body by burying it in a nice place and putting a stone with nice words on it, and flowers, too.

When the body dies, before it is buried, God takes the soul out and brings it to where He is, in heaven. The soul is us, not our bodies. Our soul is who we really are. It is sort of like what hap-pens to a hermit crab. A hermit crab will leave its shell behind, just like we leave our bodies, but the crab is the part that left the shell, not the shell.

Our soul is the part of us that goes to be with Jesus when our body dies. Our body stays back here on earth, but our soul goes on to heaven. *And that is what happened to Buddy. His body stayed here and we honored him by burying his body and putting a nice stone on it. But Buddy—his soul, the real Buddy—went to be with Jesus.*

Buddy was like a caterpillar. When a caterpillar goes into a cocoon, its body dies and stays there, but the butterfly it becomes flies off and lives somewhere else. Buddy's body stayed behind, but his soul flew to heaven like a butterfly.

Chapter 6

"Will Buddy Ever Come Back?"

Once again, before I delve into answering this question, I would suggest that you consult one of the many professional guides on child behavior and bereavement. Many offer at least a snapshot blueprint on how different age-groups perceive death.

For some age-groups, death is not viewed as being permanent. They are constantly exposed to cartoon and video-game heroes who are repeatedly resurrected to fight on. The age can vary, of course, depending on a host of maturity factors. Regardless of age, however, if your child asks a question like this, it signals that, at the very least, they embrace some hope that the return of their pet is possible.

The return of their pet is not possible. This notion needs to be nipped in the bud quickly. I am not saying we should crush their hopes, but rather that we should give them better, more realistic hopes. Our loved ones—animal or human—cannot come back to us, but one day we will go to them.

David, the king of Israel and the man whom God said was a man after His own heart, uttered those very words after his son, whom he and Bathsheba had conceived in sin, died. David said that the lad could not come back to him, but that he would one day go to his son. That is one of the pillars of faith in God: that we will be reunited with Him and our loved ones one glorious day in the future.

There is no shortage of seers and psychics who will disagree with me about our departed pets being able to return to this life. They claim that there are such things as ghost pets, apparitions, and visions, as well as psychic connections that bridge this world with the afterlife, and medium go-betweens.

Pardon my irreverence, but when I hear someone say this, I say, "Please pass the bread, the baloney has already been around." Now, I have no doubt but that many of these self-proclaimed mediums are sincere, but I also have no doubt that they are sincerely wrong.

I will not address this topic here, as it would take us far off topic and would, for some of you, be very redundant. I cover it in great detail in my book *Wagging Tails in Heaven*, which many of you have probably already read. Suffice it to say that the Bible clearly disallows any such phenomenon. There are myriad passages that address this, but essentially what God says is that once we have left this life, we cannot return under any circumstances. And neither can anyone contact us. Period!

In any event, I am certain that when children ask this question—Will Buddy ever come back?—they are asking whether he will ever come back bodily and nothing more. They are not asking if they can contact him through some medium or psychic.

The answer, though, is still a resounding "no." In **Luke 16** we are told the story of the rich man who died and awoke in hell, or Hades, and Lazarus, the beggar who died and wound up in Paradise. Hades and Paradise were located together then, but separated by a great gulf. On one side there was great suffering and regret; on the other, great bliss and joy.

To paraphrase the exchange between the rich man and Abraham the patriarch who had died many years before, the rich man asked if someone might be sent back to his former life to warn his brothers about the awful place in which he had now found himself. Abraham's response was negative. It could not be done. It was not allowed.

Do not be fooled, either, by the claims of "near-death experiences," in which people report that they left their injured or dying bodies and saw a bright light or a brightly lit figure beckoning them to come to the light. These reports are entertaining, even intriguing. It is human nature to gravitate toward seemingly supernatural and unexplainable phenomena. But do not be fooled as those making the report have been. In **2 Corinthians 11:13–14**, which warns of these beckoning figures and those whom they deceive, we are told:

> *For such are false apostles, deceitful workers,*
> *transforming themselves into the apostles of Christ.*
> *And no marvel [wonder] for Satan himself is*
> *transformed into an angel of light.*

The Lord warns us that there are false apostles and prophets who claim to be apostles of Christ, but who are actually of Satan.

Satan is called the "great deceiver" in the Scriptures. We are told that he uses evil wiles, or ploys, to confuse and deceive us. Eve discovered how effective his deceptive ways were, and after all this time, he still finds he can easily deceive human beings.

Satan and his minions can appear as angels of light, but they are not. They are so adept at their deceit, however, that good people, who have an affinity toward God, can fall for their deception and imitation. They can work through politicians, teachers, celebrities, the news media, radio and television personalities, and even those who call themselves "ministers of God" but who are nothing more than wolves in sheep's clothing.

We cannot trust anyone who ministers or teaches anything contrary to the Word of God. It alone speaks for God. It alone is God's authority. And it alone tells us, without ambiguity, that those living souls who have departed this life, human or animal, can never return.

The answer, then, to your child for this chapter's title question is, "No, Buddy cannot come back." But we can temper the sting of that answer by assuring our children that we will one day go to be where he is.

What to Share with Your Child
QUESTION: *"Will Buddy ever come back?"*

This will be a very short answer, because the Bible gives us the answer to this question right away. Now, don't be upset at the answer, because it may not be what you want to hear, but there is a lot of good news that goes with it.

First, to answer your question, Buddy cannot come back. Now, wait, don't be sad about that. He probably wouldn't want to come back anyway. He misses us and wishes he could see us, but it is so nice there in heaven that he just wouldn't want to leave. And besides, he knows that one day, even though he can't come back to us, we will be able to go to where he is. One day we will be in heaven, too.

Don't be upset that he doesn't want to leave heaven. He is so happy to be young and healthy again, and to be in a place where everything is beautiful and there are no troubles. I think we can understand his wanting to stay there, right?

There are a lot of people who don't like where they live and so they move. And there are people where they moved to who don't like it there, and so they move somewhere else. People are always leaving different places here on earth because they don't like certain things about those places. But no one has ever left heaven because they didn't like it. They love it there. So, why should we want Buddy to leave heaven, where he is so very happy?

Besides, I think God wants Buddy to stay, don't you? If He didn't, He wouldn't have brought him home to heaven in the first place.

Let's be happy that Buddy is happy now. And his happiness is so complete. He is in a wonderful place where there is no pain or old age. He is young again, and he is able to run and jump and play. And he knows that his family will one day join him. Wow, won't heaven be great?

Chapter 7

"Did It Hurt Buddy to Die?"

O death, where is thy sting? O grave, where is thy victory? The sting of death is sin, and the strength of sin is the law.
—1 Corinthians 15:55–56

You are probably thinking that this well-known verse about death and the grave would fit better in chapter 1, where I actually discussed death. You might be right, but I purposely avoided using it there so that I could apply it to this chapter to make an important point.

I think it will serve a better purpose here as we answer this question about pain. My reasoning for this will become clear later in this chapter. I will defer discussing this passage until then.

While death may be a difficult concept for some children to completely grasp, pain is not. Everyone has experienced pain, even the very young, and experience is always the best tutor.

Pain is something children know about, so don't misunderstand their question. They do not want to know what pain is, but they want to know whether their best friend suffered from it when he/she died.

Let me reach back into chapter 1 for a moment, as it is closely related to what we are discussing here. The question that children most commonly ask first, after the passing of a pet (or a human relative) is, "What is death?" Again, young children do not completely or accurately understand death. There are probably many reasons for this, but two of the most significant reasons are:

- 🐾 Most of them are shielded from it by their parents and by society.
- 🐾 The entertainment industry tends to misrepresent death, implanting in children the bogus view that death is temporary and reversible.

Despite this shielding and the gross misconceptions fed to them by the entertainment media and video games, kids still have an awareness of death. Relatives die. People whom they or their parents know die. They hear about death on the news or overhear adults talking about it. And they see that adults are upset by it, so when they are confronted with the death of a family pet, they are suddenly touched by the reality of it, and they ask for clarification so they can better understand it.

But children never ask the question, "Mommy, what is pain?" They already know the answer. It is something that has touched them many times, and they want nothing to do with it. It is undesirable, and they may even fear it. Even the most minor "ouchies" can make most kids cry and carry on for some time.

Pain is something children want Mommy or Daddy to stop right away when it happens. With even the most miniscule scrape or the tiniest splinter, anything else that Mommy is doing must stop until this life-shattering medical emergency is remedied. Usually, the only medical attention required is a small Band-Aid, a kiss from Mother on the "boo-boo," or an encouraging "There, that ought to do it," to make the world right again. But you wouldn't think that would be enough by the way they carried on before receiving Mom's miracle cure.

Companies that produce Band-Aids understand this common mind-set of children and that this age-group is comprised of the customers who use their product the most. That is why they offer their products in such colorful assortments, with happy faces and catchy designs on them. When shopping with Mommy, the kids gravitate toward these Band-Aids, because they are eye-catching and look "cool."

Mom likes them because her child likes them. He asked for them, and when the time comes to use them, she will be able to remind him of that to reduce the chances of yet another wrestling match to apply one to the latest cut or abrasion. It makes her job as the household paramedic that much easier.

So, pain is a big-ticket item for children. They have experienced it, they don't like it, and it scares them. This fear is seen at home, at school, or at the doctor's office. The first thing they ask at the doctor's office is usually "Will it hurt?" It doesn't matter what "it" is. They might be there for an annual examination, an X-ray, or the dreaded immunization booster shot. It doesn't matter; they are very apprehensive about pain. Their only concern is whether whatever is going on will hurt them.

So, it is only natural for children to be a little anxious as to whether their best friend was in any sort of pain when they passed. As tough as it might be to have to field this question, it should be refreshing to see that your child is developing a sense of compassion and care for the suffering of others.

That notwithstanding, this question places a pretty big burden on parents, especially if the family pet did die tragically and unexpectedly. If death came as a result of injury or accident, talking about whether they felt pain or not is going to be difficult. Injury or accident usually means trauma, and you probably won't be able to hide the fact that pain was present.

As we discussed previously, children expect us to be up front and open with them, and doing so really bears better fruit in the long run than any other tactic. One word of caution: We need to be honest with them, but we do not have to be *brutally* honest. Not all the facts or information about a severe injury need to be relayed to your children. Spare them any ghastly details. Please be discerning in that regard, remembering their tender hearts.

Now then, moving along, I have performed a great deal of research on the matter of pain and the way animals react to it. I didn't say that I performed exhaustive research, so I am not claiming to be an expert on this topic. But I am sure that I have thought about and studied animals and their response to pain much more than the average person.

Much of what I have read on the subject amounts to little more than the subjective opinions of both professional and non-professional people who work in the animal services industry. But when I join that information with my own observations and the experiences of literally thousands of readers who have shared their stories with me, I think I have gained a pretty good understanding on the subject.

Then, when I consider all of that in the light of our biblical text in this chapter, **1 Corinthians 15:55–56**, I think we can draw some pretty solid conclusions about death and pain. The verse doesn't actually address pain, but there is a correlation there, if you will humor me for a moment as I try to build my case for you.

There are different levels of awareness of life. If I take an ax to a troublesome tree root in my yard, the tree does not try to dodge the blow of the ax when I swing it. Its level of awareness does not allow it to "see" the blow coming.

If I swing the same ax at my dog (and, of course, I would *never* do such a thing—this is *only* for illustration purposes!), my dog would jump quickly to avoid being struck. Animals have a keen self-preservation mechanism in their makeup, as do we humans. They will flee or fight to preserve their lives.

In my studies, coupled with the observations and accounts shared by readers, I have come to believe that animals face death differently than we humans do (and I will explain this more fully in a moment). As a consequence, their reaction to pain seems quite different, as well. Let me explain.

That animals have a self-preservation mode they go into when faced with danger is commonly known. They will do whatever it takes to escape and survive attacks from predators or threats from the environment, such as floods or fires. However, when an animal is mortally wounded by a predator or falls ill with a terminal illness, it appears that they are able to accept their fate much more readily than humans. And they do so with a re-markable sense of peace.

When ill and dying, it is commonly reported that animals do not show a fear of death. Admittedly, this is not empirical evidence, but example after example has been shared with me by readers that support this conclusion. I have also witnessed this peaceful behavior in my own animals as they succumbed to untreatable ailments.

For a very long time, I wondered why this was so. Certainly humans, who are able to reason and analyze far better than the most intelligent animals, should be able to understand and accept impending death better than an animal. We are logical, pragmatic beings given to linear thinking. But the evidence suggests that none of that matters; animals seem to accept death much more gracefully than humans do.

Humans react quite differently to death and pain than animals do. Few humans accept their fate and just give up. Our intelligence motivates us to defy death. We seek second opinions and revolutionary cures. We try to pump up our resolve and determination by saying things like, "Cancer isn't going to beat me," or "I'm not going anywhere."

Such resolve is great. Projecting a positive and persevering attitude is wonderful. But the downside to all of this is that it displays, even emphasizes, our fear of death. And let's be honest: We do fear death. That fear is universal. It transcends gender, race, age, and any other socially dividing factor you can name.

Our biblical text for this chapter explains why this is so. Let's look at it again so we can discuss it.

O death, where is thy sting? O grave, where is thy victory? The sting of death is sin, and the strength of sin is the law.
—1 Corinthians 15:55–56

We are told that the sting of death is sin. This word, *sting*, is a Greek word that means "to prick" or " to stab." When you are pricked or stabbed, it causes pain. So we can safely say that what it is saying here is that the pain, or hurt, of death is sin or, presumably, that sin is what makes death so painful.

It can be complicated performing word studies in Greek. Often, you must exegetically look at many other associated passages to determine what is being said, and that can increase the difficulty factor for you. But I did the work on this one, and it all boils down to this: People fear death because of sin. Sin is the "stab," because we know that sin is disobedience and rebellion against God and His laws.

A human faces death, and their soul is discomfited by the thought of death because of sin. There is a mysterious component to death, a fear of the unknown, of the perceived darkness. This is the sting of death at work. Even believers, who, by virtue of the atonement of Christ, are assured a place in heaven, struggle with this "apprehension."

Animals, however, have no such fear. The reason for this is because they have no sin issue to deal with. They are sinless, innocent creatures. There is no sting in death for them, nothing to unsettle their souls. Because death does not hold the same dread for them, it follows that they are not spiritually anxious and not feeling the "pain" of death.

Even when death is not impending, the pain threshold for animals is amazing. I could bore you with countless stories of the strength and stamina of these noble personalities we call "pets," but I don't think you need any convincing. You probably have as many stories to share as I do. It is well-known and commonly accepted that animals handle death and pain far better than the average human does. Some might balk at that statement, but that is a preponderance of the opinions I have researched, not mine alone.

Given all that we have covered here, I believe that the approach parents should take in answering this question for their children is clear. I would begin by explaining to them that God never wanted any of His creatures to feel pain. He did not want sickness, pain, or death to come upon any of us. But because of sin, people and animals feel pain. We get sick. And we die.

And while it wasn't the innocent animals that sinned, they still suffer under the curse brought on by the fall of mankind, as does the entire planet. And the curse is that the bodies of all living things age, feel pain, and die.

In spite of that curse, it appears that animals do not feel pain as badly as we humans do. The reason for this is not clear, but it might be that because they are innocent and sinless, God treats them in a special way and helps them through their pain. It doesn't embarrass me to speculate on this, because I learned a long time ago that God is fair and that He does some pretty extraordinary and wonderful things behind the scenes.

In closing, a good portion of this chapter was offered to help those who have lost pets under tragic circumstances, such as an accident or injury. My hope is that only few readers need this help, and that most of you are using this guide because the family pet passed on due to age-related issues, and thus without much pain.

Accordingly, the "what to share with your child" narrative below will address losing a pet due to age, not other tragic circumstances.

What to Share with Your Child

QUESTION: *"Did it hurt Buddy to die?"*

I am going to answer your question in just a moment, but first I want to make sure you know that God never wanted Buddy to suffer with pain. God didn't want any animals or people ever to be in pain, or ever to be ill or die.

But when sin came into the world, all these bad things came with it. Animals and people feel pain now. They get sick and sometimes they die. But, honey, you shouldn't worry about whether Buddy suffered in pain or not. I don't think that it hurt at all when Buddy died.

I think we all know that it was hurting him to live. His old body was just so sore that it was hard for him to stand and even harder for him to walk. That is why we had the veterinarian give him medicine to help take away some of the pain.

You know how Mommy sometimes gets a headache, and when I take an aspirin, it helps to take away my pain? That is what Buddy's medicine did for him. After he took it, the pain went away for a little while and he could stand and walk.

But the medicine only lasted for a while, and then the pain would come back. And after a while, the pain started to get worse and worse and the medications weren't helping anymore. But you know Buddy—he didn't like to complain. Sometimes he would cry a little when it hurt a lot, like when he had to walk, but even then he was always wagging his tail for us.

Still, sometimes he just didn't want to get up, and when that happened, Buddy would look up at me with those great big, sad eyes as if to say, "Can't you do something to help stop this pain?"

Do you remember when you stepped on that nail, how it hurt and how you screamed and cried? It was a sharp pain that really hurt, didn't it? But in a couple of weeks, it healed and felt better.

Buddy's pain wasn't like that sharp pain you had, but it hurt just as much. Buddy's pain was a dull, aching pain that would never heal, and it was there all the time, day and night.

Now, Buddy wasn't in any more pain when he died than he was when he was alive. But when he died, he didn't hurt more—he hurt less. And now he doesn't feel any pain at all because he is in heaven.

I am thankful to God for ending Buddy's pain and for making him young and healthy again. Aren't you?

Chapter 8

"DOES BUDDY KNOW THAT I LOVE HIM AND MISS HIM?"

Oddly enough, this question is asked more by adults than children. But I suspect that the number of adults who ask on behalf of their children is significant enough that this question should be included as part of this guide.

This inquiry is quite unique from others that are posed. It just does not always ring true. There seems to be something not being asked, something ulterior. I believe that more often than not, this question is actually a "mask" question. By that, I mean that it intentionally hides or obscures the issue that is really on the mind of the person asking the question. The truth is that when this question is posed, it is usually spawned by regret for something that the questioner did in the past, something to do with their pet.

Think about it for a moment if you would. Why would anyone who opened their home and their heart to an animal, who fed and cared for it for many years, who walked it in the rain and the snow, question whether or not their pet knows they loved them? Absent mitigating factors, the answer should be obvious to them; "Of course they know that."

But there are obviously underlying concerns that prompt this question. The only logical explanation is that the person is worried about something negative that might have occurred between them and their pet, and they wonder if that plays into their pet's overall memories of them.

If that seems far-fetched, let me assure you that it is not. I speak from personal experience. I was haunted by this very thing, regretting just one instance of negative behavior toward my best friend and wondering if she had ever forgiven me for it.

When I unexpectedly lost my wonderful sixteen-year-old West Highland white terrier, Samantha, I was heartbroken. In fact, I was devastated. But something that overshadowed even my pain was my regretful memory.

Just months before we lost Sam, our family went on a short road trip. We had been driving for a while and everyone was tired, so we stopped near an open field so that I could stretch my legs and walk the dogs. It was a semi-country area with a few buildings around, but otherwise pretty secluded, so Sam was allowed to be off her leash. She never wandered far from me anyway, so there was no danger.

Sam did her business, and then began reading the "doggy newspaper" (i.e., the grass, where dogs leave and receive social news for each other). I stretched my legs, and while doing so, I noticed a small pond to my left with a little island in the middle of it.

Someone had laid a large log down from the shore to the island to serve as a bridge. Actually, I suppose it would be incorrect to call it an "island," because it wasn't actually surrounded by water, but rather by mud. And it wasn't really mud, either, but more of a bog. And it was that really putrid, yucky stuff—the black, gooey, smelly kind of bog that comes from decaying and rotting vegetation.

I decided to stretch my legs a little more by walking across the log to the island while Sam finished investigating the grass. The log bounced wildly from my weight, but I managed to cross it without much problem. As I did, I thought to myself, *Hey, I would do pretty well on one of those lumberjack challenge shows.*

When I got over to the island, I discovered another way back to the car via dry land behind some nearby bushes. So I headed off in that direction to circle back to the car. What I didn't realize was that as soon as I disappeared behind the bushes, Sam got anxious and started after me—or at least to where she had seen me last.

My wife, seeing Sam's reaction to my going into the bushes, called out and alerted me that Sam was coming my way. I knew she would not use the log to get across that bog, so I quickly yelled loudly from inside the bushes, *"Sam, stop!"* I had to yell loudly, because old age had taken away most of her hearing.

But she heard me and she stopped immediately, just inches from the bog. Sam was such a good girl. She always did what she was told—that is, if she understood you. I had her stopped, but then I made a mistake. I should have come out of the bushes and given her hand signals to move back, because she had learned to respond well to visual prompts since her hearing loss.

Instead I yelled, *"Go back!"* I don't think she heard the "back" part, because she went in the wrong direction. She had heard "go," and that was a green light for her to come my way. And, of course, she never did anything halfway; she jumped right into that awful, decomposing swamp and struggled through eight feet of bog, coming out on the other side looking more the color of her shadow than herself.

She stunk so badly that even the flies wanted nothing to do with her, and we had to get back on the road, which meant that we had to all get back in the car. And this is where the seed for my future regret was planted. I was so upset that I scolded her, loud enough so she could hear. I knew she heard and understood, because her ears went down and she lowered her gaze.

I looked around in desperation for some idea of what I could do, and miraculously I spotted a faucet and a hose on one of the nearby buildings. I led Sam over and gave her a long, thorough bath. I wasn't gentle, either. I scrubbed and scrubbed until I finally brought her black color to a middle brown, and then we doused her with hand lotion and perfume, trying as hard as we could to mask the smell.

Unfortunately, it didn't help much. We had to drive the remainder of the way home with the windows all cracked open, which made it noisy and hot. And when we got home, Sam got yet another rough bath, because the whole ordeal still had me upset at her.

The point to this long story is that when she passed, this one memory came flooding back to me. Instead of remembering the sixteen years of love and care I gave her and all the moments we spent enjoying each other, I was focused on those short fifteen minutes of impatience I had with her. It caused me such pain and regret that it haunted me for many months.

I would have done anything for a do-over, but that would never come. It took a long time before I could allow the good memories to finally win out and put the bad moments in context, but it finally happened. But I learned a very valuable lesson that I hope you pick up on here, and that was that I would never "lose my cool" with any of my pets ever again.

For the record, this one unfortunate incident aside, Samantha was otherwise a very happy dog. She lived the life of a princess in our home. She was loved and pampered her whole life. We planned vacations around her, purchased homes with yards to accommodate her, and basically let her run our lives. And I do not regret a single moment of our time with her, other than that one slip on my part.

I believe that it is very important to evaluate all the questions your children ask you, in an attempt to discern what prompted their curiosity. But this question, in particular, suggests that there may be something they did concerning their pet that they feel guilty about now. It doesn't necessarily even have to be anything bad. Again, children have tender hearts, and even the smallest matter can impact them in a big way.

Guilt is a serious issue for anyone, child or adult. It would be advisable to gently prompt them to share whatever it is that is bothering them. You may get them to open up by simply asking them straight-out if something is wrong.

If that doesn't work, you might try a less direct approach. For instance, you might say something like, "Honey, I wonder, too, sometimes if Buddy knows that I love him, because sometimes I scolded him for not listening and I wonder if he was hurt by that. Do you ever feel bad like me, because you did something you wish you hadn't done?"

If that doesn't get them to open up and share with you, then maybe there isn't anything to share after all. I would not worry too much about it. You might revisit the issue during the evening devotions provided for your use, or you might just make a mental note to talk to them again about the issue in a day or two. Whatever it takes for you to ensure that they are not harboring feelings of guilt or regret, take the time to do it.

Alternately, proceeding as if the question is just an earnest concern asked without ulterior motives, it is important that your children do have the assurance that their best friend knows that he is loved and missed. We could discuss the helplessness and hopelessness that children feel that spark questions like this, but I think that would be stating the obvious to you. Instead, let's move right to the suggested narrative to use with them. I have found this approach to be very effective for readers and their families.

What to Share with Your Child

QUESTION: *"Does Buddy know that I love him and miss him?"*

Honey, this question worries me a little, because it sounds like you feel like Buddy doesn't know that you love him. I am certain that he knows, but I do understand how you can worry about that.

I wonder, too, sometimes if Buddy knows that I love him, because sometimes I scolded him for not listening, and I wonder if he was hurt by that. It makes me feel bad. Do you ever feel bad like me? Why would you think Buddy might not know that you love him?

Give your child time to answer. Be patient and try to just sit quietly. Sometimes the silence will move them to talk to you. And of course, respond to any response with great understanding and compassion. Then continue.

You know, there are millions of other dogs, and cats, and other animals, who don't have a home or who don't have people who love them. Buddy had a family who loved him and who gave him everything he needed. He knew that we loved him.

He always got treats. He always had someone in the family playing with him or petting him. I think you are worrying for nothing, because Buddy knew he was loved very much. In fact, if Buddy could write us a letter from heaven right now, I bet he would say something like this:

> *Hi, everyone. I just wanted to write and tell you how much I appreciate the love that you all showed to me. I was so happy to be part of our family, and one day we will be together again. I always felt so safe and so loved in your home. And I loved it when someone would just sit and stroke my fur and talk to me. I felt so important and so loved. Thank you, thank you, thank you.*

> *I am sorry I had to leave, but you know that I was getting very old and doing things was just getting so hard for me. Here, I don't have any pain and I am young again. I can run*

*and jump and roll around. You will be so happy when you see
me again one day.*

Mother talking again:

*Now, honey, I know it hurts to think and talk about Buddy so
much like that, because we do miss him. But I had to say all of
that so that you would know just how Buddy feels. He knows that
we all love him. And he knows that we all miss him, too.*

Chapter 9

"WHAT IS HEAVEN LIKE, MOMMY?"

As you might imagine, there are a lot of ideas floating around about what heaven is like. Everyone has their own theories and ideas about it. This is one "religious" topic that almost everyone is willing to talk about. I would presume that is because the thought of heaven carries with it a very positive connotation and makes people feel good about the future.

Many of the ideas and concepts that people have are so outrageously foreign to the Scriptures, they border on being ridiculous. One woman claimed that God is a big ball of energy and that heaven was like an electric grid. Another said that heaven was like a big spiritual airport where all souls are cleared to land. Their ideas are kind of amusing, but not at all accurate.

There are even those who claim to have visited this place via Transcendental Meditation, cosmic projection, or some other pseudo-spiritual means. When pressed for a description of heaven, they cannot tell you what it looked like, but when you quote a detail from the Bible, they are quick to say, "Oh yes, that's right, I saw that." Pleeeeeeease!

A trip to the Christian bookstore can prove to be just as humorous. On a recent visit I picked up several books about heaven to skim through. The first thing that caught my attention was that these books were approximately four hundred pages long, and some much longer. That struck me as funny, because if we were to combine all that the Bible has to say about this wonderful place, we would have perhaps ten pages of typed words.

So what could these authors possibly find to write about? I have to confess, I don't know. After reading about the shopping malls and movie theaters that would be there, I kind of lost interest and put the books down. It was literary swill, with no biblical basis. But you will find that that New Age, feel-good philosophy has found its way into many books supposedly about the Bible, so this should not be surprising.

Theologians agree that heaven is a spiritual place. I largely agree, but I am not convinced that this is the whole story or the best description. This conclusion is largely based on circumstantial evidence (i.e., it cannot be seen, contacted, etc.). We cannot dial up the Hubble telescope and focus in on someplace billions of light-years away. We cannot dial 411 and find a telephone contact number for someone living in heaven.

So, since we cannot see it, and because we cannot make contact with anyone who dwells there, we feel that it can't be a physical place. It must be a spiritual locale, unreachable from a physical plane. But for me, that doesn't work. Simply labeling heaven as "spiritual" is just not an adequate description for me.

There are other considerations relative to what we are told about this place, but we give them little or no thought, because it is not a convenient time to do so. Heaven is far off in our minds, and we still have a lot of living to do. Most people just don't give heaven much thought until they are in the winter of their lives.

Labeling it as a spiritual place, however, effectively removes it from a person's reality radar. This is probably why there are those who just do not care very much whether it exists at all; they have postponed thinking about it for so long that it has become relatively unimportant to them.

Don't misunderstand me: I am not rebelling against this commonly accepted position of heaven being in the spiritual realm. I wholly agree with that assessment. I am merely saying that I think there is more to the story. I am certain that while we view this place as being in a spiritual dimension, for those who presently dwell there, it is as physical a place to them as earth was before their passing.

That is a fact easily ascertained from the Scriptures. People who have passed from this life are physical beings, not spooky, ghostly figures or unexplainable floating orbs. One good example (of the many that we could point to in the Bible) is found in the book of Luke, chapter 16. The scene we are afforded a glimpse of takes place in Hades. Let me say right up front that this is a true-to-life account. It is not a parable. The characters in the story are real people. They were once alive on earth, and they are alive now in Hades. One of the characters, in fact, is a well-known Bible figure: Abraham.

At the time of the story, Hades consisted of two independent compartments: Hades, where the unbelieving dead were placed, and Paradise, the peaceful place of rest for those of faith. Paradise is no longer a part of Hades, as those who were there were relocated to heaven upon the resurrection and ascension of Jesus Christ.

Briefly, Luke 16 tells us that there was an unbelieving rich man who was being tormented in the flames of Hades. Seeing Abraham afar off on the other side, in Paradise, the man called out to him. He asked Abraham if Lazarus, a beggar whom the rich man had seen on earth, might dip his finger in water and come to quench his thirst. Abraham advised the man that those in Paradise could not help those in Hades, because of the physical barrier between them. There was no way for Abraham to send Lazarus, because of the gulf between them.

Every element of this story speaks to the fact that the afterlife is a physical place. These people had physical bodies. They felt physical thirst, as well as physical and emotional pain. They were limited in their ability to move by physical obstacles.

There are myriad scriptural examples to support the fact that heaven is, in and of itself, a physical place. How it can be spiritual and physical at the same time remains something yet to be understood, but God does not always explain things to us. Rather, He expects us to accept what He says as true. This is called "faith." Faith is simply taking God at His Word, with or without the empirical evidence that science demands.

It seems prudent to identify which heaven we are talking about. The Bible speaks of three heavens. Respectively, they are: the immediate atmosphere surrounding the earth; the universe beyond the earth's atmosphere; and the place where God dwells.

This third place is the place we traditionally refer to as the heaven where we all want to go, the final resting place for believers. However, there are actually two such places mentioned in the Scriptures. The first is the present heaven, where God, His angels, and departed saints (believers who have passed away) reside at this very moment.

The second version of that heaven is not yet in existence. It will be the "new heaven" or "New Jerusalem," which we are told about in **Revelation 21:1–2**. The apostle John was moved by the Holy Spirit to write:

> *And I saw a new heaven and a new earth: and*
> *the first heaven and the first earth were passed*
> *away, and there was no more sea. And I John saw*
> *the holy city, new Jerusalem, coming down from*
> *God out of heaven, prepared as a bride adorned*
> *for her husband.*

Some are confused about this place called the New Jerusalem. They think it is a temporary abode for the redeemed. It is not. This cubical city is the new heaven, or the New Jerusalem, and it will be the permanent dwelling place for the Bride of Christ. We will occupy it exactly 1,007 years from whenever the rapture of the Bride of Christ, the Church, occurs.

It will literally be heaven on earth. Well, perhaps heaven "near" earth would be a more accurate description, as we are told this great holy city will sit literally in the sky above earth. Yes, I said it will sit in the sky, or the clouds, and the only reason I say that is because God said it will sit there.

Now, I understand that this sounds almost like something from a fairy tale. The first time I heard this, I, too, was quite skeptical. But having studied the topic for so many years, there can be no doubt that God means exactly what He said. This city will sit in the clouds. This was confirmed to John by an angel in **Revelation 21:9–10**:

> *And there came unto me one of the seven angels which had the seven vials full of the seven last plagues, and talked with me, saying, Come hither, I will shew thee the bride, the Lamb's wife. And he carried me away in the spirit to a great and high mountain, and showed me that great city, the holy Jerusalem, descending out of heaven from God.*

The dimensions of this holy city are gargantuan. It will be a hundred times the size of the original and current city of Jerusalem here on earth. Roughly, its three-dimensional measurements will be 1,500 miles long, 1,500 miles wide, and 1,500 miles high: a cube. It will cover 2,250,000 square miles, roughly one-quarter the size of the contiguous United States.

Artists' conceptions of this cubical city on the Internet look strangely similar to the Borg cubes we were introduced to in several of the *Star Trek* offerings. Perhaps there will be some similarity in general shape, but undoubtedly the similarities end there. It will be a breathtaking city devoid of any of the ills we see in earthly cities or the industrialized wasteland on the imaginary Borg cubes.

The streets will be paved with transparent gold in the purest and most precious form. The gates and other internal structures will be decorated with precious stones that will project a regal brilliance. The city will dazzle onlookers and draw eternal praise to the Architect who designed and prepared it.

There is so much more that could be said about the New Jerusalem, but since it will be more than one thousand years before we get to see it, I suppose it can wait. I think it is more important that we move on to describing the current heaven, where we go to now when we pass from this earth and where our reunions will take place.

The actual size of this heaven is unknown. We are not given any specific information regarding its size. However, I think it is safe to make an assumption regarding the size. And before I do so, let me say, "Yes, I know the old joke about what 'assume' means."

I don't know what knucklehead came up with that cliché joke, but there is nothing wrong with making an assumption based on the facts available. An assumption is a guess—nothing more. God has given us logic and the ability to deduce. Drawing conclusions is a necessary and natural function.

And so, I am assuming, based on the facts available, that heaven must be a rather huge place. It may not be as large as the New Jerusalem will be, but I suspect that it is. In fact, I am certain it is a grand place on every possible level. Let's not forget that the inhabitants are the redeemed (those who put their trust in God) from every dispensation of mankind's history. The total population could easily number in the billions.

Regardless of size, the regal décor will undoubtedly reflect the majesty of the Most High. Kings on earth spared no expense to ensure that they were surrounded with the most beautiful and breathtaking trimmings. God the Father, at no expense to Himself, will decorate the home of His only begotten Son's Bride, in never-before-seen splendor.

And the accommodations for those who are called after His Son's name (Christians) will not be shabby. God is not going to have tenement housing. Our presence with Him for all eternity is a big deal to Him. It seems to me that our reunion with God is looked upon with as much joyous anticipation on His part as it is on ours. So, when He said that He would prepare a place for us, irrespective of whether it is in the current heaven or in the New Jerusalem, I am sure that He has spared no luxury.

God does not do anything small. He parted the Red Sea for His chosen people; He didn't send a boat or make them walk around it. He did it purposefully and in a big way—so big that it is talked about even today. He rained fire down on Sodom and Gomorrah; He didn't send eviction notices or just turn the power off. It was a spectacularly big event. So it is pretty safe to assume that when it comes to size and beauty, He did not cut corners in heaven.

If we are not thoroughly overcome with the vastness of God's universe and His heaven, then surely the beauty of heaven will do the job. Everyone has a picture in their minds as to what heaven may look like. Without exception, I am confident that this picture is one of beauty in everyone's mind. We are talking about heaven, after all, one of the few topics that is always referred to in a positive light, along with babies, puppies, and kittens.

In **1 Corinthians 2:9**, God tells us:

> *Eye hath not seen, nor ear heard, neither have entered into the heart of man, the things which God hath prepared for them that love him.*

God only hints at the beauty of heaven, but He does so in a very poetic and intimate way. Embodied in the glimpse He gives us is an assurance of the love He has for us. Jesus Himself told us before He departed that He was going to prepare a place for us, and here God alludes to the sheer wonder and beauty of that place.

But He guards His words, so as not to give away too much detail. It is almost as if He doesn't want to spoil the surprise He has for us. And isn't that how you act when you love someone and want them to be happy with what you have done for them? You cover their eyes and guide them into another room, where you have that beautiful cake or spectacular present waiting for them.

There is also a good probability that if God were to reveal the details of heaven to us, we would not be able to wrap our finite minds around them. When the apostle John saw the Lord Jesus in His glory in heaven (see Revelation 1:17), he fell down as a dead man. The sight was too much for him to absorb in his present state.

The apostles John and Paul both reported that they were restrained, or otherwise supernaturally prevented, from sharing some of what they were told by the Lord or by angels to others. It is likely that what they were told could not be easily understood or accepted. Indeed, they themselves struggled with it.

But not knowing every minute detail about this destination called heaven should not be a discouragement for us. Jesus told us not to fear or to worry: He would ensure it was ready for us and that it would be a place better than any other place we had ever seen before or could even imagine.

Even conceding that there are not a lot of details provided in the Bible in terms of what heaven is like, there still is much to glean from our text. First, we are told, "eye hath not seen. . . ." Think of what this means. No living human has ever seen anything as beautiful and as wonderful as this place.

As I have mentioned elsewhere, Hawaii was my home. The Aloha State is undoubtedly one of the most beautiful places on earth. The *mauka* (mountains), *aina* (land), and *kai* (ocean) combine with the constant blue sky to enchant all onlookers. Most of our scenery, particularly on islands other than Oahu, is simply breathtaking. There is beautiful scenery on Oahu, too, but overcrowding and expanding highways and industry have robbed the island of much of the beauty that it once had.

The beaches of the islands come in a variety of colors: white, tan, black, and red, for example. Often, these beaches leave an indelible impression on visitors, and they become walking advertisements for Hawaiian tourism back on the mainland. It is not uncommon for first-time visitors to make it a special point to ask tour guides to show them these beaches.

Over three thousand species of birds serenade those who spend time outdoors, even at the tables of outdoor restaurants, where they will befriend you for a few crumbs of bread. And whether outdoors or in, one cannot mistake the fragrant bouquet of our vast variety of flowering plants, wafting everywhere on the gentle trade winds.

There are times when the fragrance of night-blooming flowers, which we locals call mock orange or night-blooming cereus, coupled with a full moon shining through the soft Hawaiian clouds, intoxicates strolling lovers. Many a proposal has been generated

under the influence of that heavenly fragrance and the enchant-
ing Hawaiian moon.

But as beautiful as Hawaii is, eyes have seen it. Eyes have seen
Angel Falls. Eyes have seen the Napa foothills in California. Eyes
have seen the White Cliffs of Dover. But eyes have never seen
anything like the beauty that God has prepared in heaven for
those who love Him. Earth's beauty spots are memorable, but
they will pale in our memories when we behold the splendorous
beauty of heaven.

This first part of our passage (i.e., "eye hath not seen . . .")
causes me to think fondly of the late Frances Van Alstyne, blind
hymn writer and wonderful Christian woman. You might recognize her better by her adopted name of Fanny Crosby.

Fanny was a persevering spirit. She had actually been born
with sight, but an eye ailment had taken her vision before she
was two months of age. Despite her challenging condition, she
wrote more than eight thousand Christian hymns that have been
sung by literally hundreds of millions of voices. And that is probably an understatement. Some, like "Blessed Assurance" and "Pass
Me Not, O Gentle Savior," have endeared themselves to countless generations of believers.

Despite her many noteworthy accomplishments, the thing I
remember best in Fanny's biography, however, was an answer
that she gave to someone who asked her the question, "If you
could change anything in your life, what would it be?" Obviously, this person was sure she would answer with the answer
that most anyone else in her condition would: "That I could see!"

But surprisingly, that was not Fanny's response. Her answer

was that she wished that she had been blind from her birth. I know that may seem like a strange response from someone who was blind almost all of her life, but I assure you that it was a well-considered answer on her part. Though she had been blinded as an infant, she had constant recollections of two faces, a man and a woman. Presumably, they were the faces of her parents, who had hovered over her crib so many years ago.

Her love and devotion for the Lord Jesus was so perfectly selfless that if she could have changed anything in her earthly life, it would have been that the first face she ever saw in her existence would be the face of Jesus. This was not grandstanding on Fanny's part. Her gentle and humble spirit was real, and it often manifested itself in the hymns of praise and worship that she wrote.

Her wish was impossible to grant, of course, but that is of no consequence, because since 1915, Fanny has been enjoying that face of the Lord she so longed to see.

The next portion of **1 Corinthians 2:9** says, "nor ear heard. . . ." Essentially, this means that no human being has ever been able to come back from the dead and report on the beauty and wonder of the heaven that God has prepared for us. The Lord repeatedly makes brief mention of the place, but again, never with great detail.

This portion of the verse speaks also to our having never heard the beautiful sounds and songs of heaven. We know that there will be a choir there, but our only experience with choirs on earth may not allow us to absorb and appreciate the perfect blend of melody and harmony there. I do not mean to be cruel, but I have heard some choirs that were nothing to write home and tell Mother about. In fact, the choirs of several of the churches I attended had choirs just like that—especially after I joined them!

Whatever awaits us, I am certain that our ears are in for a treat. Music on earth is inspirational and moving. In heaven it will undoubtedly take on new dimensions of holiness and beauty that will live up to the claim of this verse.

Moving on to the final offering of this verse, it says, "neither have entered into the heart of man." What exactly does that mean? It speaks simply of our imagination. We are assured that the wonder and beauty of this place, heaven, is so far above anything seen on earth that in our minds we could not even conjure up something that resembles it. Our finite minds have not happened upon such beauty, not in a dream, not in a daydream, not even with our creative imaginations.

Our imaginations can create new thoughts and images. There is almost no limitation as to what an active, vivid mind can dream up. My emphasis here is on *"almost,"* as we do have one limitation: We can only draw upon the experiences of this earth-locked life that we now live and the few things not of this world that God has chosen to disclose to us in His Word.

Our experiences are governed by our senses: what we have seen, touched, heard, tasted, and smelled. Since our imaginations can only draw upon the three-dimensional (or four-dimensional, if you count time as a dimension, as some do) experiences we have had, the perception of a multidimensional heaven is outside of our capacity.

We may think that our ideas are wild, insightful, and even revolutionary, but God dedicated an entire book of the Bible to remind us that "there is nothing new under the sun." It was true in Solomon's day when God inspired him to pen those words, and it is just as true today.

We are finite, limited beings. Our imaginations are limited. Not only have we never seen or heard of anything like the beauty of heaven, but if we deliberately attempted to stretch our imaginations to that high level, our faculties would fail us.

There is so much more we could discuss about this place called heaven. We have not even touched upon the wonders of this place, the absence of time, or the presence of almighty God there. Unfortunately, this chapter is already far too long, and it is time to conclude our answer to this question.

In summary, I have no doubt but that we will literally and involuntarily gasp out loud when we are whisked away to this blessed place and behold its beauty. We will stand silently in awe at the wonder and spectacle of heaven and the majesty of God.

What to Share with Your Child
QUESTION: *"What Is Heaven Like, Mommy?"*

Oh, that is a wonderful question. Isn't it exciting to think about heaven and what it will be like? God has made so many promises to us about this place. Here are just a few of the things that we know:

 🐾 *Heaven will be a place of happiness. There will be no sadness or crying. No one will get angry at anyone else. No one will get sick or die. There will be nothing to be unhappy about.*

- 🐾 *Heaven will be a place where we see old friends and loved ones. Buddy will be there, and you will be able to spend as much time with him as you want.*
- 🐾 *Heaven is where God is. You will get to meet Him for the first time, and it will be such a wonderful meeting.*
- 🐾 *Heaven is a place without time. Now, that is hard to imagine, but there will never be darkness or night. The day will never end. There will be no clocks or bedtime.*
- 🐾 *Heaven is a place where we never grow old. It will be nice not to have wrinkles or to feel aches and pains like me and your dad sometimes feel.*

*In **1 Corinthians 2:9**, God tells us:*

> *Eye hath not seen, nor ear heard, neither have entered into the heart of man, the things which God hath prepared for them that love him.*

Wow, God says that heaven is so beautiful and so wonderful that no one has ever seen anything like it before. Do you remember when we were at the Grand Canyon last summer? Wasn't the scenery just so beautiful? Of course it was. But God says that heaven will be much more beautiful than that. I can hardly wait to see it.

Then God says that we have never heard anything like what we will hear in heaven. I am not sure what this means, but I think it is talking about the music we will hear up there. It will be so beautiful and so sweet that it will make us happy all the time.

Finally, God tells us that heaven is not like any place you have ever imagined. It is better. We can imagine some really nice things, can't we? I was thinking just now of living in a beautiful house next to a babbling brook with flowers growing all around it. The water is so clean that I can just reach down and scoop some up and drink it.

That is a nice thought, but God says that thought is nothing compared to what He has planned for us in heaven. And you know what? Our Buddy is enjoying all of that beauty and wonder right now! He is so lucky, isn't he?

Heaven is going to be a really nice place for us one day. I am looking forward to it, aren't you?

Heaven is so beautiful and wonderful. . . .

Chapter 10

"Will I Ever Go to Heaven, Mommy?"

Such a question should stop you in your tracks. It should move the earth under your feet, along with your heart. Is there anything a child could ask that is more innocent or compelling? This inquiry should strum the heartstrings of any parent and touch them to their very soul.

Here is their cherished child asking about their own mortality. They may not be asking it directly, but there can be no doubt but that they are thinking about what happens after this life. They are acknowledging it out loud to themselves, and causing you to confront the stark reality that they will one day die. How could anything be more somber and heartbreaking than this?

Of all the things in this life that have caused me pain and regret, nothing has been harder for me to bear than watching my adult children age. Of course, I don't plan on being here when it happens, but knowing my children will one day pass on tortures me emotionally. If it were possible, I would divide my remaining years between them to add a few more years to their lives. But, of course, that isn't possible.

The best thing I could do for them actually proved to be the best that I could ever do for them, better than anything else I could have done. That was to ensure they knew about God and had a personal relationship with the Lord—and they do. They never had to ask me whether they would go to heaven one day, because they already knew they would. This life will end for them, and there is nothing their old dad can do about that. But they are assured of the next life by their faith in Jesus Christ.

As easy as it may sound for me to have shared the gospel with my own children, there is much more to the story; it was not easy at all. Oh, their part was a breeze. All they had to do was hear Dad out on what the Bible said and then believe. Children have very little difficulty in accepting the things of God. Mine were no exception.

It was I who was the problem. Before my children would hear the gospel and respond, I had to come to a place in my own life where I did business with God, and did it His way. As some of you may know, that is a lot harder than it sounds.

I was a religious person. I believed that Jesus was the Son of God. I believed in the Father, Son, and Holy Ghost. But I could not buy in to the idea that there was only "one way." There were so many other people in the world who didn't believe what I believed. Were they all wrong?

Couldn't it be possible that when people worshiped Buddha, they were actually worshiping my God? Couldn't it be that the Muslims and Hindus and all the other faiths of the world were actually worshiping the same God whom Christians were worshiping?

I thought it was at least possible. And while I was not a fanatic or a religious activist over the matter, that was the way I believed. I sort of bought in to the Baha'i faith outlook, which basically teaches that religion is the way to bring unity and fellowship to the entire world. It is not.

Of course, I eventually found out how wrong I was, and I am extremely happy that I did. In fact, there are times when I can sit and think about how close I was to saying "no" to the Lord Jesus, and remaining in my confused and lost religious state, and I literally shudder at that prospect.

But that realization did not come easily. It was a process, and the process started unexpectedly. I was in the United States Navy at the time. I was stationed at Commander in Chief, U.S. Pacific Fleet as the top secret control yeoman for the Pacific theater. It was a much better job than it sounds.

Hawaii was my home, so I also had many connections and responsibilities in the community. Among them, I was an instructor (Nidan) in Shodokan karate for the Japan International Karate Center, then the largest karate institution in the world. I really enjoyed my work as an instructor, but it kept me very busy, teaching every work night of the week.

I would get off work with the navy around 4 p.m., head home, gobble down the dinner that my wife had made, and then head off to teach my first class of the evening. I taught six classes each night in various locations around Oahu. After teaching, instructors were required to meet in the downtown dojo at 11 p.m. for "instructor sparring" for about an hour. Then we would cap off the day by jogging around Honolulu for an hour. Weekends were worse.

By the time I got home on weeknights, it was nearly 3 a.m.,

and I had to get up to get ready for work at 5 a.m. Often I would not sleep at all and just head back to work to start my routine all over again. It really wasn't a problem for me, because I was seldom tired and all that exercise made me an insomniac. I just could not wind down enough to be sleepy.

I share all that with you so that you can understand that my ridiculous schedule predictably caused me some marital problems. It eventually came to the point that my wife and I simply didn't know each other anymore, because we hardly saw each other. Worse, the children did not get to see much of me, either.

This is where the process I mentioned before began. Out of the blue, I began to feel a tremendous burden for my children. The best way I can explain what I felt was that I was overwhelmed with the thought that, not only was I not being a good father to them, but that I was not ensuring that my kids went to church or knew the Lord. I shared my feelings with my wife, and she confided that she had been experiencing the same burden.

I made time to talk about it with my wife by skipping my first class that evening. I knew my assistant would fill in for me at the class. My wife and I talked a long time. We didn't know how it was going to happen, but we decided to make a concerted effort to go to church or talk to our children about God in the very near future. We made no specific plans, but at least we were moving in the right direction.

And we ended our conversation with a prayer. We didn't even know how or what to pray, but we simply asked, "Lord, we want our children to grow up knowing You. Please help us with this. Amen." I then kissed my wife and told her that things would get better, and I headed off to my next class.

That class was in the city of Waipahu, at August Ahrens Elementary School. After working the class out in my usual tough manner, I gave them a much-needed ten-minute break. I decided to spend that time outside, enjoying the bright Hawaiian moonlight. As I stood there contemplating how beautiful the skies were, the sound of singing drifted across the schoolyard from a church just on the other side of the school fence.

I listened to the words that the folks were singing, but I knew that I had never heard that hymn before. As I listened to the words, they stirred me deeply. It wasn't the music or the harmony of the voices that touched me; it was the words and the sincerity with which they were sung.

I would learn later that the song was "Victory in Jesus." Years later, this hymn would become one of my favorites, as it is for many believers. But I am getting ahead of my story.

It was time to bring my class back inside. I smiled to myself for having the good fortune of experiencing that song, and I filed the experience away in my memory. I had no idea at the time how God was going to use this experience in the process that He had started in my life.

The very next day—not a week or a month later—but *the very next day*, a series of events began to take place that would change my life forever. And I do literally mean *forever*. It was the next step in the process God had put into play to meet the spiritual needs my wife and I had laid at His feet.

I was in charge of the combined federal campaign for my navy unit, which is the annual fund drive for charities recognized by the federal government. In that capacity, it was my job to make contact with every employee and ask them if they would like to donate to the campaign. It wasn't a difficult job; most federal employees anticipate the annual drive and have their donations automatically taken out of their paychecks each month. My job was simply a formality to remind them and to encourage non-participants to sign up.

When I approached a young man by the name of Larry and gave him the standard pitch, he responded with only an unexpected *"no thanks."* His response caught me off guard. You must understand that, even though contributions are voluntary, every military unit wants to be able to say that they had 100 percent participation.

Total participation reflects well on the command, and individual contributions become considerations in officer fitness reports and enlisted evaluations. I know that to call this "voluntary" in that regard seems almost humorous, but that is the way of the military. For whatever reason, this annual drive is a big deal for them. I have seen commanding officers donate a dollar in the name of people who would not contribute, just to gain that perfect 100 percent level for their command.

And that is the mentality I used in dealing with Larry. I pressed him and said, "Look—just give one dollar—so we can say we have a hundred percent participation." He said, "Sorry, no can do." I wouldn't let it go. I responded, "Not even one dollar?" He answered again in the negative.

I pressed him a little further and even tried to shame him into donating. He finally said that this month he just could not afford it, that he had given his tithe to his church and that every penny of his paycheck was spoken for that month.

When I asked what "tithes" were, he told me that a tithe was

10 percent of his pay, which God had said believers should give to the ministry. I could hardly believe what I was hearing. In fact, I didn't believe it, and I think I even called him a liar. No one would give that much money to their church!

But when I asked him to prove it, he produced a tithing receipt from his wallet. I checked the date and everything. He wasn't lying. And as he opened his wallet, I noticed that he didn't have any cash in it. He wasn't lying about that, either. So I backed off on the donation matter with him.

He really impressed me, and I wanted to know more about his beliefs and his church. Why did I want to know more? I cannot explain it, except to say that it must have been another step in the process God was undertaking to reach out to me.

This is evidenced by what I next learned. He invited me to attend his church one Sunday, Lanakila Baptist Church in Waipahu. Can you guess what church that was? That is exactly right: This man was a member of that little church outside the elementary school where I taught karate at night, where I had heard those folks singing. In fact, his voice was probably among the voices I had heard.

This revelation nearly floored me—literally. I actually got woozy. I had absolutely no way of knowing that he worshiped at that church. Similarly, he had no way of knowing that I had been listening to the singing from his church that evening. When I found out that he was a member there, the only thought in my head was the memory of my wife and I telling the Lord that we wanted our children to know Him. It was a little "spooky" for me, to say the least.

I didn't take him up on his invitation, because Sundays were very busy days for me at the dojo. But for the next several weeks, Larry and I engaged in many conversations about religion and God. Actually, it could better be described as arguing. He would tell me something about the Lord, and I would disagree. He would always respond with, "But it says so right here in the Bible . . ." It was rather frustrating, because I wasn't really keen on the Bible.

Our arguments became more and more passionate. He became bolder, and I became more frustrated. Finally, in desperation, or perhaps in exasperation, I literally picked Larry up and hung him on a clothes hook in the back room. I can still see him dangling and squawking on that hook. It seemed funny at the time, but it is a source of regret for me now.

All of our conversations culminated one morning when Larry quoted the Bible to me one too many times, and I lost my cool. I fired back at him, "Oh, quit quoting that dumb book. Everyone knows that it is full of contradictions."

By the shocked look on his face, I thought I had finally won our ongoing arguments. But I had forgotten that his talking to me was part of God's process and that God never loses. Larry looked me straight in the eye—a brave act, seeing as I might have hung him up on the hook again—and said, "How do you know that, Gary?"

What? I had expected more than that. But when I thought about what he said, his words hit me like a ton of bricks. If I am nothing else, I am an honest person. If I am wrong, I will admit it. If I do something bad, I will own up to it and take my medicine. And now I had been hit with a question that I had to honestly consider.

How, indeed, did I know the Bible was full of contradictions? I had not read it. I had not studied it. I "just knew"—but how did I know? Before I could come up with an answer, Larry added, "Why do so many people believe that?"

He had me flustered now. I couldn't think. But again he spoke and added, "Doesn't it make you think that maybe there are bad forces at work influencing people to believe a lie about the Bible?" All I could think was, *Wow!* As an honest person, my mind had been considering that possibility before he even mentioned it. How, indeed, could so many people believe the same thing without having read it? There had to be some unseen influence at work.

And so I responded, "Larry, I really don't know why I think that, but it scares me to think that my personal beliefs could be manipulated without my even knowing it—I want to discuss this with you more." And so, for the next week I allowed him to show me scriptures without arguing about them, and I found a new world of truth. I found a source of answers that I had never known existed. Oh, I knew the Bible existed, but somehow I had never recognized its authority.

I learned the Bible was more reconciliatory than judgmental. It did not condemn me, but it told me that I was condemned already—and that the Lord had taken deliberate action to help me, to reconcile me with Him. Larry did not indoctrinate me. He merely answered the questions that I asked and pointed me to the basis for his answers in the Bible. I read it for myself and drew my own conclusions.

To bring this long story to an end, in about a week I came to the point that I realized I needed the Lord in my life. I thought

I had known Him, but I had only known *about* Him. I had never placed my personal trust in Him or recognized that He was the only Way.

Up to that point, I was one of those who thought, *There are many paths, but they all lead to the same God—surely God recognizes the intent of men and women to know Him.* But the more I explored the Bible, the more I realized that God never meets men on their terms or by their devices, but rather when they yield themselves to His way.

All this acknowledgment and understanding manifested itself on my bathroom floor a short time later, where alone I knelt in prayer and said, "Lord, I had not realized how far I was from You. I thought I believed in You, but now I see how much I truly need You. I am sorry that Jesus had to die for my sins. I accept what He did and accept Him as my Lord and Savior."

In an instant, everything was different. Everything was in correct perspective. I realized the realness of God, I knew the love of God firsthand, and I knew that I now belonged to Him and that nothing in life or death would ever pose an eternal threat to me again. It was an amazing experience, as if I had awakened from a deep sleep into a world of understanding.

It was clear to me that God had honored my desire to know Him and had set in motion a series of events to bring that to pass. And He didn't stop there; He has walked me carefully through my life since then.

Just two short years after that day when I heard those Christians singing, I became a deacon in that same church. Another two years passed, and I filled in as interim pastor for a couple of months while we waited for a new pastor to arrive.

From this process that God initiated at my request, my eternity was settled. Shortly after this, my wife and children took care of business with God, too. And our lives together changed. I gave up karate. I shocked everyone—even myself. I had just won the All Hawaiian Open Karate Blackbelt Championship and was nationally rated. I had a great future in martial arts, something I had always wanted.

But my heart had literally changed overnight. My priorities had changed, too. Leading my family to a better life in the Lord and serving His interests instead of my own became more important to me than anything else.

Previously, my religious compass had been broken. I had so many wild and wrong ideas bouncing around in my head that it is amazing that God was able to get through to me at all. With children, however, we have a clean slate to work with. There are no erroneous views to contend with or to wipe clean.

Your first priority in answering any question that your child asks is to ascertain exactly what your child means. Remember, kids do say the darnedest things, so the question might mean something completely different from what you suspect. But taking it at face value, it appears that your child wants to make sure he will one day be where his Buddy is.

Accordingly, you need to explain their spiritual need for God to them. I would strongly recommend that you approach this the same way my wife and I did, through prayer. Ask the Lord to lead and to take control, and you simply cannot go wrong.

I have selected **John 14:6** for our text for this chapter to help you with this responsibility. I did so, because if I had known this verse during the time I was so confused, it might have rescued me a little quicker than my rescue was actually effected. So, why not start your children out with it from the start? It reads:

> *Jesus saith unto him, I am the way, the truth, and the life; no man cometh unto the Father, but by me.*

Note that Jesus didn't say He was "a" way, but "the" Way. What a marvelous distinction. He removes all doubt and ambiguity. He is *the* Way, *the* Truth, and *the* Life. No one else can claim that there is another way to heaven than through Jesus. Any other way is not *the* Way, but a false way that leads not to the Father, but away from Him.

What to Share with Your Child
QUESTION: *"Will I ever go to heaven, Mommy?"*

When you ask me this question, it makes me wonder why you asked it.

Are you asking about heaven because you know that is where Buddy is and you want to make sure that you see him one day, or are you wondering whether God will let you go there one day?

Give your child time to express what they are thinking. Chances are, they will just shrug and say, "I don't know," as children commonly do.

Well, I suppose it doesn't matter why you asked the question, because the answer is the same for any reason. Anyone who wants to go to heaven can go there when their life here on earth is over.

They just have to be right with God. Do you know what that means? Let me explain.

When Adam and Eve chose to disobey God, they sinned. They were not right with God. Sin is when people do or think bad things. God is good, and He does not like for anyone to do bad things. He does not want sin around Him. When people do bad things, they are acting like Adam and Eve and sinning, and that means they are not right with God.

And what did God do to Adam and Eve when they had sin in their lives? That's right: He made them leave the Garden of Eden. Now, that Garden was like heaven for Adam and Eve. But they could not stay there because they had done bad things.

Everyone does bad things or thinks bad thoughts. Everyone has lied. Everyone has disobeyed their parents. Everyone has gotten angry, or has wanted what someone else has. God calls all of these things "sins." When we have sin in our lives, we are not right with God.

And, you know, there is no one who is right with God. God doesn't want our sin in His heaven. So He made a way for us to get rid of that sin and to be right with Him. He sent His Son, Jesus, to pay the price for our sin. You know the story of Jesus and how He died on the cross.

In the old Bible times, before Jesus came, the people of God had to sprinkle blood so that God would forgive their sins. The Bible tells us that only the shedding of blood will pay the price for sin. So, Jesus came to shed His blood for us so that we would not have to do it. He did it for us.

God said that if we want to be right with Him, now all we have to do is believe in Jesus and ask Him to forgive our sins. When we do that, the blood of Jesus covers our sins in God's eyes. We are forgiven, and we no longer have sin controlling our lives. Then we are welcome in heaven when we die.

Now, Buddy didn't have to believe or do any of these things, because animals do not sin. Did you ever hear Buddy lie? No, of course you didn't. Did you ever see Buddy steal? No, he never stole anything. Animals do not sin. So they are welcome in heaven.

But each of us as people need to believe what God tells us in the Bible about sin and about going to heaven. You have heard the word gospel before—do you know what it means? It simply means "good news."

The gospel is the good news that God sent His Son, Jesus Christ, to die for our sins so that we could be forgiven and be with God in heaven one day. The good news is for people—all people every-where. All they have to do to make sure they have a place in heaven is to believe what God said and ask Him for forgiveness.

Do you believe what God said:

🐾 That you are a sinner?
🐾 That Jesus is God's Son?
🐾 That Jesus died for your sins?
🐾 That you need to ask for God's forgiveness?

Then let's bow our heads together right now and ask God for forgiveness. Now, I already did this. I already asked Jesus into my heart a long time ago, and people only have to do it once, so I don't need to do it again.

But I can help you. Would you like me to help you? I can pray with you and say the words, and then you can just repeat them *with me. But you have to really mean them. Do you really believe in Jesus, and do you want to ask Him to forgive you? Then, let's pray together.*

After praying:

Now, wasn't that easy? God makes it so easy for us to be right with Him. Doesn't it feel good knowing that we have done what God wanted us to do, and that we are right with Him?

Now we need to start spending time as a family learning more about God. We are going to begin having evening devotions soon. That will be a time when we talk about God and try to help each other feel better about Buddy going to heaven. It will be very good to learn some of the things God wants us to know. It will help us feel happier.

Chapter 11

MISCELLANEOUS QUESTIONS

There are other questions that children commonly ask that do not require much background to answer. I was tempted to call them "lesser questions," but decided against doing so, because I did not want to give the impression that they are not as important. If a child asks one of these questions, it is just as important to them as any of the others to which we have dedicated an entire chapter.

The dozen questions that follow do not make up a complete list by any means, but apart from those we have already addressed, these are questions that I have fielded more frequently than others when communicating with readers. Theoretically, then, they should be the most common that you will encounter.

As you will undoubtedly notice, some of these questions have been indirectly answered in other segments of this book. I will include them here, however, and address them more directly so that you don't have to search them out or deal with incomplete answers.

The format for this chapter will be slightly different than the others. I will simply present the question and then provide a scripturally based suggested narrative answer to use with your child, inserting a scriptural reference, when appropriate, for your use if you need it.

Here is a snapshot of the questions addressed in this chapter for your quick reference.

- Why do animals and people have to die?
- Why do good people die?
- Why can't God just take all the bad people away and leave the good ones here?
- Why couldn't God bring heaven here so no one has to die?
- Where is heaven anyway, Mommy?
- What are angels?
- I see angels on television and they seem bad sometimes. Should I be afraid of them?
- Do angels die?
- Is Buddy an angel now?
- Do you think Buddy has angel friends?
- What is Buddy doing right now, Mommy?
- Will we get old and die again in heaven?

Question: *Why do animals and people have to die?*

Do you remember the story about Adam and Eve? They were the first people to ever live. God gave them a beautiful garden to live in. This garden was like heaven on earth. There was no sin, and because of that, there was nothing bad in Eden.

Adam and Eve sat and petted the lions and bears. They proba-

bly swam with the alligators. Animals did not eat meat back then, only grain and vegetables. And they were all tame. Think about a great big bear playing with you like Buddy did when he was a puppy. That was how all animals were back then.

The bees did not sting, the ants did not bite, and spiders were not "icky." You could hold a bee in your hand, and it would have hummed in pleasure like a cat purrs now. Every animal and insect lived off the things that grew in the ground that God created.

But we are told in the Bible (**Romans 5:12**) that sin came into the world by Adam and Eve, and we know it was when they disobeyed God. And the Bible tells us that because of that sin, everything in the Garden of Eden changed.

Animals became meat eaters, and some had to run from the others because they would be eaten. And all animals had a fear of people come over them. That is why animals usually run when you see them in the woods. They are afraid of us.

The bees started stinging, and the ants started biting. Spiders starting making webs to catch other insects, mosquitoes started to bite, fleas began biting dogs and cats and other animals. Everything changed for the worse.

And then the Bible tells us in **Romans 5:12** and **James 1:15** that sin caused everything to start dying. Flowers started to wilt in the sun, insects were caught in spiders' webs, lions began eating their prey, and every living thing began to age.

Adam and Eve started to show the marks of age. There were wrinkles under their eyes, their hair started turning gray, and they started to feel aches and pains, like headaches, toothaches, and tummy aches.

God didn't want it to be this way. He made Adam and Eve and

all the animals, insects, and plants to be perfect so that they would live forever without aging or illness. But God gave Adam and Eve free will. That means they were able to make their own choices and decisions.

Even when God knew it was the wrong decision for them to make, He didn't stop them, because He kept His promise to let them choose. He told them it was the wrong decision, but they did what they wanted to do anyway.

That is why sometimes when your father and I know you are making the wrong decision, we tell you it is wrong, because we want everything to be good for you in your life. But sometimes you have gone ahead and done what you wanted to do anyway. Then, when you find out that your dad and I were right after all, it is too late.

Remember that time when you said that you could jump over the fence in the backyard, and we told you that it was too dangerous? You tried anyway, and you got hurt. You found out too late that Dad and I were right.

Well, Adam and Eve did what they wanted, even though God had warned them not to. They found out that God was right. But it was too late; the damage was already done. And as a result, the whole world changed and God made them leave the Garden.

People and animals die because people did not listen to God and sin came into the world and brought death with it. God didn't want this to happen. But now that it has, He has fixed it by sending His Son, the Lord Jesus Christ, to die for everyone.

People still die in this life, but because of what Jesus did, we now have a new life waiting for us when we leave this life on earth.

Question: *Why do good people die?*

God tells us in **Romans 3** that there is no one who is truly good. In His eyes we are all sinners. Everyone has told a lie. Everyone has been angry and said to or thought bad things about someone else. We have all disobeyed our parents. So, really, we all have sinned.

But in our eyes, there are good people and bad people. Some people do more good things and some more do bad things. When you helped me carry in the groceries, that was a good thing. When a man robs a bank, that is a bad thing.

God knows that, but when it comes to people going to heaven, God says we have all been bad, because He sees all the little sins, too. And we learned earlier that God does not like any sin. He doesn't want any sin in heaven, big or little.

So, even though people like us do good things and we are nice people, we still die because of sin. No matter how good they are, because of sin, all people die.

Question: *Why can't God just take all the bad people away and leave the good ones here?*

You have to remember that God said He loves the whole world (see **John 3:16**). He loves everyone the same. We may not. We may look at bad people and not like them. But God loves them. He looks at the bad things that they do and He hates those bad things, but He loves them as people.

When He sent His Son, Jesus, to take away our sins, that made it possible for everyone to be good in His eyes. When we believe in

Jesus and accept Him as our Savior, He takes those sins away, and guess what happens then?

The Bible tells us that He throws them away forever, and God the Father forgets all about them. They no longer exist. God will never think about them again. All He will think about is that we have put our faith in His Son.

Remember a while ago when you got angry at Mommy and you said that you didn't love me anymore? I knew you didn't mean it, but you were having a bad day and you were in a bad mood and you got angry.

Later on you felt bad and came and told me you were sorry. And what did I do? Did I tell you it was too late? Did I tell you to move out of the house? No, I forgave you, because I love you. And not only that, but I forgot all about it.

That is what God does. When we tell Him we are sorry for the bad things we did and we ask His Son into our hearts, He forgives us. And He also forgets our sins.

So there really are no "good" or "bad" people in God's eyes. We are all sinners who need to ask for His forgiveness. And when we do—even people whom you think are bad—He forgives us and forgets about our sins.

QUESTION: Why couldn't God bring heaven here so no one has to die?

This is a very good question, honey. I am so glad that you spend so much time thinking about things like this. It shows me that you really like to think things through.

It seems like it would be so nice if God could do that, doesn't it? But let's think about it for a minute. Why does God not live here? What is the one thing that God hates so much? That's right, sin. And this world is full of sin. People are doing bad things all the time. Do you think God would enjoy Himself here?

Now, in heaven, it is so peaceful and wonderful. There is no sin there. There are no lies. No one steals. No one sins. Just think about all the things that we have here on earth, that are not needed in heaven:

- *There are no doctors (because no one gets sick).*
- *There are no locks (because no one steals).*
- *There are no fire extinguishers (because there are no out-of-control fires).*
- *There are no cemeteries (because no one dies).*
- *There are no policemen (because no one breaks the law).*
- *There is no hunger (because God takes care of everyone and gives us all food).*
- *There is no fear (because God protects us all).*

And there are a thousand other things that make heaven such a better place to live than here. Let me ask you: Where would you rather live, in your room with all your toys and things, or outside in the woods? I know you would rather sleep in your nice, warm bed than on a pile of old wet leaves outside.

God is just like you in that way. Why would God want to be here with all this sin, when He has such a wonderful place to be in heaven? Aren't you glad that instead of coming here, He invites us to come there to live with Him in that wonderful place?

QUESTION: *Where is heaven anyway, Mommy?*

Where do you think it is, honey?

(Give them time to respond and then continue.)

Well, you might be right. I don't know. No one really knows where it is. Jesus said in **John 14:3** *that He was going there to prepare a place, so that when He came back for us, or when we die, we would have a place to live there. But He didn't tell us where exactly it was that He was going—only that it was heaven.*

Most people think it is a spiritual place that we cannot see, and I guess that is what I believe. But life is as real there as it is here. There are people alive and living there right now. There are animals and angels there right now. Just because we cannot see it, that does not mean it is not real.

It is kind of like the wind. You can't see the wind, but you know it is there. And it is kind of like love, too—you can't see it, but you can feel it. So, heaven is like that—we can feel it and we know it is there, because the Lord said it was real and we believe Him.

Wherever heaven is, it is a place of great peace and beauty. It is a place without sin, where nothing bad can happen. But more importantly, it is where Jesus is. That fact alone should make us want to be there, no matter where it is.

I am reminded of the story about a local pastor who was visiting a man in the community. The pastor had brought his dog with him to the man's house, but left him outside to wait for him. As he told the man about the Lord and heaven, the unbelieving man asked rather sarcastically, "Well, if you know so much about God and this place called heaven, tell me what it is like there. What is it like on the other side?"

The pastor confessed, *"Well, I don't really know. I only know that God said it was wonderful and I am looking forward to going there."*

The man said, *"What? You don't know what is on the other side of death, and yet you trust God to go there?"*

Just then the pastor's dog, whining and crying impatiently, scratched on the outside of the home's door. The pastor reached over and opened the door, and the dog came springing in and rushed quickly to the pastor's side, licking his hand.

The pastor turned to the man and said, *"Did you see what my dog just did? He has never been in your house before. He had no idea what was on the other side of that door or what awaited him. He only knew that his master was here, and when the door opened, he ran in without fear or hesitation. I know very little about what is on the other side of death, but one thing I do know is that my master is there, and that is all I need to know."*

Question: What are angels?

Angels are beings that God made before He decided to make people. We aren't told a lot about them, but we know that there are several different types of angels in heaven. There are seraphim, cherubim, and archangels. Each has different jobs that God gave them to do, but all serve God faithfully.

There are other angels that rebelled against God and sinned. They are no longer in heaven. They are called demons, and their leader is Satan. These are not faithful angels, and one day God is going to punish them, but for right now He just keeps them from causing trouble in our lives.

Angels are strong and powerful beings that God used to do special things. They are stronger than even the superheroes in the movies, but angels are real, not make-believe. Long ago, in Bible times, God used angels to do miracles and to bring messages to people on earth. Today they serve God in heaven, but they can also serve as guardian or guarding angels for Christians.

Just like we cannot see heaven, we also cannot see angels, unless they allow us to. But they are always here helping believers to be safe. Sometimes they can be seen (**Hebrews 13:2**), but we do not know that they are angels. They may take the form of people to do God's work, and then they leave without anyone really knowing an angel was there.

QUESTION: *I see angels on television and they seem bad sometimes. Should I be afraid of them?*

What you see on television is almost all make-believe. "Make-believe" means that it is not real. Hollywood is a place where people create make-believe stories. They make television programs, cartoons, and movies about things that are not real. They do that because it is entertaining to people, and because people will pay money to watch things that entertain them.

There are some bad angels in the world, but as I explained earlier, those angels are in trouble with God. They have sinned against Him, and He will judge and punish them one day. Until then, we are told that they are kept out of heaven in chains, but that they can sometimes bother us on earth (see **Jude 1:6** and **2 Peter 2:4**).

The other good angels—and there are a lot more of them—are in heaven, and they would never do anything to harm or hurt people. They are sent to earth by God to be our guarding angels. Their job is to watch out for our safety and well-being.

There are many people who can tell you stories of being helped by angels. Some of the stories are hard to believe, but if we believe in God and that He sends angels to help us, we can believe them by faith.

Here is a story that I know to be true.

(Story 1 is for older children only—for younger children, Story 2 would be a better option.)

Story 1

Do you know what a missionary is? A missionary is a preacher who goes to another country to tell the people there about God. This story is about a missionary who took his family to a very wild place in the jungle.

The missionary was told that the native people were very mean and that they might hurt him and his family, but the man felt that God wanted him to go and talk to these natives, so he did. When he met the chief of the tribe, the chief told him to leave the jungle or he and his family would be killed. The chief told him that they would play drums all night, and that when the drums stopped, the warriors would come with spears to kill the missionary and his family.

The missionary and his family were not afraid. They went to their tent and prayed together all night for the Lord to protect them. As they prayed, the sound of the drums grew louder and louder and was so frightening. Then, after hours of beating, the drums suddenly stopped.

The family waited for the warriors to come as the chief had threatened, but they did not come. In the morning, the missionary went to the chief and asked why he had changed his mind and not come with his warriors to kill them.

The chief said in sloppy English, "Me no change mind. Warriors come, but fiery warriors in your camp too many, too strong, we no can fight. Your God too powerful. Now you tell us about Him."

It was clear to the missionary that God had posted angels that appeared to be fiery warriors around his camp, just as He had done in the Old Testament for one of His prophets.

Story 2

A young boy and his father were canoeing down a river that turned unexpectedly and treacherously wild as they came around a bend. The river had met a large tributary stream that had swollen from rains upstream. The father fought with all his might to keep the canoe steady, but after hitting a rock, both he and his son were thrown from the small boat.

The father tried to swim to his son, but the wild current carried him out of reach and quickly whisked him downstream. The boy had a life preserver on, but the father knew that there was a very dangerous waterfall about a quarter mile downstream.

Struggling with all his might, the father made his way ashore and began running down the shoreline as fast as his legs would carry him. He crashed through bushes and leaped over rocks without allowing them to delay him, but despite his efforts, he lost sight of his son.

As he came to the last bend before the waterfall, his heart sank as he realized he was too late. As he prepared to dive into the water and go over the waterfall himself in a desperate effort to save his son, he heard a voice to his right call out, "Dad, I'm okay! I am over here."

Relieved, he ran over to where his son was sitting on a rock and said, "Oh, I am so glad you managed to pull yourself out, son!" His son responded, "No, Dad, I wouldn't have made it if that man had not helped me."

His father said, "What man? I didn't see anyone. Where is he?"

The son replied, "He was in a blue suit. He was just here. He went over . . . well, I am not sure where he went. But if he hadn't pulled me out, I would have gone over the waterfall."

The father did not know what to think. What would a man in a blue suit be doing out in the wild? And where did he go? There was no way out of the river valley, except the way he had come while running toward his son, or over the waterfall. He didn't know what to think.

But his son expressed what they both suspected, "Maybe he was an angel, Dad?"

Then return to your response to the question:

The angels of God are good. They serve Him and protect His children. Don't let the things that Hollywood says make you fear angels.

QUESTION: *Do angels die?*

No, angels do not die. They are eternal creatures, just as people and animals are. But angels already live in heaven, so they can never die. People and animals must go through death in order to get to heaven.

Death is a door to heaven for us, but angels do not need a door, because they are already there. They do not die. They do not get sick. They never tire or get old. They are living the eternal life that you and I will one day have, just like Buddy is living now.

QUESTION: *Is Buddy an angel now?*

No, Buddy is not an angel. He never will be. Animals are animals, people are people, and angels are angels. I know that sometimes in the cartoons and movies on TV it shows that people become angels when they die. So it is natural to think animals might, too. But they don't—and people don't, either.

Angels were created long before people and animals. Once God finished making the angels, that was all there would ever be. There would not be any more. Angels do not create other baby angels. There are not male and female angels. They are given male names like Gabriel and Michael, but they are not male angels. They are just angels.

People have babies. There are male people and female people. Animals have babies. There are male animals and female animals. But angels are not male or female. So, they don't make baby angels, and there can never be any more than there are right now.

And people and animals cannot turn into angels any more than animals can turn into people or people can turn into animals. We *were made differently by God, and we can never change who and what we are.*

But we will live together with the angels and worship God together in heaven. I am sure that we will have all sorts of angel friends in heaven one day.

QUESTION: **Do you think Buddy has angel friends?**

Of course, Buddy has angel friends. In fact, he probably has so many angel friends you couldn't count them all. You know how everyone who met Buddy when we walked him just loved him? Well, since heaven is so much better, we have to believe that all those there—angels, humans, and other animals—are going to want to be friends with Buddy.

Based on many things that the Bible says about the next life, when people and animals get to heaven, we believe that God gives us all more knowledge and awareness. We will know people and animals that we never met before, and they will know us.

When you have a group of your friends together, say for a party or for a school field trip, you have a lot of friends and you all get along. But someone almost always manages to say something bad or make someone else upset eventually.

Heaven won't be that way. Everyone will get along and love each other all the time.

QUESTION: **What is Buddy doing right now, Mommy?**

That is a question I may not have the right answer for, because there is no way that I could know what he is doing right now any more than I know what your father is doing right now at work. I know your father is working, but I don't know what exact work he is doing. He might be on the telephone, or he might be in a meeting.

And with Buddy, I know some of the things he will do in heaven, but I don't know what he is doing at this very moment. Maybe he is talking with an angel. Or perhaps he is sitting at God's feet and enjoying fellowship with His Creator.

He could be out running with other dogs, too. He might be just sitting and thinking about how nice it will be to see us when we get there.

Whatever he is doing, we know some things for sure:

- He is young again.
- He is not sick anymore.
- He is not tired.
- He is happy.
- He has seen Jesus.

We couldn't wish anything better for Buddy. God has taken care of all of his needs, and Buddy is happier than he has ever been before.

QUESTION: **Will we get old and die again in heaven?**

No, we will not get old in heaven, and we will never die again after we are there. In **John 3:16**, we read these words:

> For God so loved the world, that he gave his only
> begotten Son, that whosoever believeth in him
> should not perish, but have everlasting life.

This verse tells us two very important things. First, if we believe in Jesus, we will never perish, which means that we will never die in heaven. We will have bodies that do not age or get ill. Our bodies will look like our old bodies from back here on earth, but without all the things that were wrong with them.

The teeth we are missing will be replaced. If someone lost an arm, that will be restored. If you lost your hair, you will have a full head of hair again. If someone has cancer, it will be gone. No illness will be permitted in heaven.

Then second, we are told we will have everlasting life. What does everlasting mean? It means "lasting forever." Our life cannot and will not end. We can never get old. We can never die after we reach heaven.

Chapter 12

PREPARING YOUR CHILD
FOR THE LOSS OF A PET:
EUTHANASIA

Euthanasia, by a very wide margin, is the most frequently addressed topic by readers who contact me. Easily, that figure is 20 percent. Of these, approximately half are inquiries that are posthumous, or after the pet has passed. The other half consists of people who have not yet been forced to make this very tough decision, but who anticipate that they will in the very near future, due to the failing health of their family pet.

Invariably, the 50 percent who contact me after their pet has been euthanized are seemingly motivated to do so by a sense of regret or guilt. They have read one or more of my books in this genre or heard about me from friends, and they see me as a potential source of comfort or understanding. And I do not mind that. I regret the reason that they feel the need to write, but I am happy to be of help if I can.

The questions that are commonly asked capture the essence of the guilt and regret these pet owners are experiencing. Here are a few examples:

- 🐾 Do you think I did the right thing?
- 🐾 Do you think I waited too long?
- 🐾 Do you think I didn't wait long enough?
- 🐾 Does my pet know that I love them?
- 🐾 Do you think that my pet suffered?
- 🐾 Was I just being selfish?
- 🐾 Do you think my veterinarian made a mistake?

These, and other questions like them, are most difficult to answer. For one thing, I have extremely limited information and insight into the inquirer's situation. The only thing I know about them, their pet, or their experience is what they divulge to me in their short inquiry, and that is almost never enough for me to offer any specific advice or comments.

The other factor that makes it difficult to answer such inquiries posthumously is that the writer is usually very distraught, even inconsolable, and I have to choose the words of my response very carefully to ensure I do not add to their grief. Seeking more information for them to have later on is not an option; readers expect a response that will help them right away.

Almost without exception, they confide in me that they sought help from family and friends without success. Most tell me that they even sought spiritual guidance from their minister or pastor, but again, without success. In fact, they report that quite often, instead of support, they received callous and unsympathetic responses like, "Oh, it was just a cat. Go get another one."

It is difficult for some people to understand how animals can be of such importance to people who keep and love pets. But it really isn't that difficult to explain. An animal may start out as a visitor to the home, but they almost always quickly become a full-fledged member of the family. They are not "like" members of the family, but they *are* members, and they are equally loved by all.

They develop personalities and behaviors that endear them to and complement other family members. They are unassuming, unpretentious, and dependable. They are always there for us. They do not care if we bathe or have bad habits; they love us without conditions. When we come home from a hard day at school or work, they are there to greet us and to make us feel important.

For children, the family pet can be their closest and dearest friend. They are confidants who will sit and listen when no one else will. All the while they will purr or thump their tails on the floor to show their enthusiasm. A very strong bond usually develops between children and the family pet.

For adults, our pets are perpetual children. They are our children, because they depend upon us for all of their needs—food, shelter, medical attention, etc.—and they are perpetual, because they never grow up and leave the nest. They do not marry. They do not go off to college. They remain utterly dependent upon us throughout their entire lives.

When our children leave home, we still love them and help them when they need it, but generally they have their own lives to live and we no longer make decisions for them. But for our furry children, the decision-making responsibilities remain with us permanently. They continue to depend upon us for everything, for life. Is it any wonder, then, that when the day comes when we must prematurely hasten their passing, we will blame ourselves or feel guilt? Somehow we feel we are responsible. We should have known better or done more.

Old or young, the questions above reflect the typical mind-set of people who have had to make a decision to put a cherished pet down. I hope that you never find yourself in that position, but the chances are that one day you will. You will then have to make that dreaded decision for your pet and then follow through. And worse, you will have to explain that decision to your children and walk them through the whole heart-wrenching process, as well.

Now, optimally, we want our children to know what is happening. We may not want to include them in the decision-making process, but they should be informed. Of course they will protest and beg you to find another way. They will go immediately into denial, and they may even blame you in some way for what is happening. These reactions will be short-lived and they will pass.

But I believe it is prudent and wise to let your children know what is going to happen. If the medical situation allows, bringing them into the loop will give them some time to accept and adjust to the impending loss, rather than to let it just happen without any awareness on their part. If you opt not to tell them, expect that inevitably they are going to ask you how long you knew about their pet's medical condition, and there will eventually be an emotional price to pay.

Making such a decision is one of the most difficult things a person who loves animals will ever have to do. If we allow ourselves even to think of the possibility of this happening, it usually brings overwhelming sadness. And if we dwell on that thought, as many of us do, it looms over us like a dark cloud on our horizon.

When that fateful day arrives, the questions I listed above are the types of questions you will be haunted by, first from that little voice within you, and then from those little voices outside of you: your children. Being caught unprepared will only exacerbate the trauma you and your family will feel. So you need to be ready.

You may not agree with me right now about how you will feel should you be forced to put your pet down, and you may be right. But experience has taught me that more often than not, people who love and keep pets, and who have to make life-and-death decisions for them, come to regret their decisions in pretty short order. Often, they regret it to the point of serious guilt and depression.

That doesn't mean that they *should* feel guilty. Of course they shouldn't. It is just the nature of people who love animals to feel somehow that they could have done more. "Pet people" have great big hearts, and those hearts break in a great big way when they lose an animal for any reason. And often our broken hearts lead us to second-guess our actions and intentions, which, in turn, fosters feelings of guilt and regret.

Rather than presenting you with a "what if" scenario on euthanasia, let me approach this subject as if you have already made that difficult decision to let an ailing or aging pet go. Your veterinarian advised you that there was nothing more to do for your pet, and that postponing the inevitable would only result in more pain and suffering for the animal and for your family.

Reluctantly, you make arrangements to let him/her go. You

tenderly share the sad news with your children, answer all of their questions, and spend the evening consoling them. The questions they ask will probably not be difficult, especially if you had previously discussed and explained the situation to them. You might expect questions at this time such as, "Did it hurt for him to die, Mommy?" or, "Did you get to tell him good-bye?"

And then it is time for you to face your own emotions. You look at the empty pet bed, you hear your child(ren) softly weeping in their own beds, and you finally have the time to break down and drop more tears than you thought you had in you.

Everything that has happened, every consideration you weighed, all the advice you received, it all comes flooding back to you. Without warning, you start to wonder whether you did the right thing. The wondering turns into questions: *Should I have waited a little longer? Maybe if I had pushed him, the veterinarian could have found another way?*

Please, if you glean nothing else from my extensive experience in these matters, take this to heart. In all probability, you will find yourself in more pain and grief than you would have ever imagined you could feel over an animal. You will feel that you have somehow betrayed that loving pet that had placed all of its trust in you, and you will begin to experience intensifying guilt.

As reported by many readers, and as I mentioned earlier, you will find yourself desperate for help. You will reach out to family and friends, but you will find that few understand what you are going through emotionally. It may even seem like they don't really care, because they do not place the same importance on a pet as you do.

You may also contact your minister, in hopes that he can provide spiritual support and answer some of your questions. But again, you will probably find a lack of understanding and compassion. The failure of my fellow ministers to respond positively and helpfully to their congregants, especially regarding the loss of a pet, is one of the most common complaints I get from readers.

This is precisely why I have included this chapter in this book. I want to offer that help that you will seek and need—before you need it. What follows should help readers put their circumstances and emotions into proper context.

Again, I caution you, if you feel that you are in need of professional counseling, please seek that counseling out. There are many good therapists who specialize in bereavement due to the loss of a pet. I am offering you help and insights based upon many years of experience with tens of thousands of readers. Specifically, I want to share with you how we worked together to put their feelings of guilt into proper perspective and context, allowing them to persevere over guilt that they should not be experiencing.

When we are forced to make that awful decision, because circumstances or a medical prognosis dictate that it is more humane to end a pet's suffering rather than to let it continue, doubts and guilt are going to creep in. Even though we took all the necessary safety precautions, fed them the best food, got them regular checkups, and did everything humanly possible to ensure their good health, bad things can still happen. We cannot foresee the future, and we certainly cannot change it.

Still, in our minds, we feel that we should have been able to change the outcome. We feel as if we have failed our pets. They depended upon us, and somehow we let them down. Somehow we should have had control and been able to prevent their illness or injury.

The truth is, however, we have no control over such things. We cannot know when illness will strike. We cannot know when an animal will dig a hole under the fence and run into the street. We cannot know our own future, let alone theirs.

There is no basis for feeling guilty when unexpected circumstances force us to decide to help our best friend pass on. There is no reason to torture ourselves with regrets and second-guessing. We *did not* fail them or let them down.

Think about the special love that you and your family have for your pet. Think of all you did to keep him/her safe and well. People like you and me have a special place in our hearts for our pets. There is probably nothing we would not do for them if it is within our power. When such love is present, can there be any doubt but that we would never do anything but good for our pets? Where, then, is there room for guilt?

I know when I lost my precious Missy, it was like a spear had gone through my heart. I mentioned Missy in *Cold Noses at the Pearly Gates*. She was a puppy when I wrote that book. Her antics and unrestricted devotion to me helped me weather the loss of several other pets at that time. Missy lived for sixteen years and suffered greatly from kidney failure in her last year with me. Despite all the veterinarian's efforts and all the money we spent to help her, we ultimately had to let her go.

I miss her terribly, as you will miss your own best friend. But I feel no guilt for helping her pass, because she needed and depended upon my help. There is no question in my mind but that I did everything within my power to extend her sweet little life. Her devotion to me was matched only by mine to her. People laugh when I talk about her and I say, "If I could have given her ten of my own years, I would have gladly done so," but I sincerely mean that.

I am sure that, on some level, you worry about having to face making a life-and-death decision for your own pet. If you are like the rest of us pet lovers, and I suspect you are, when that time comes you will explore every other option before you decide.

You will do everything in your power to extend the life of your best friend. I can attest to the fact that many readers who have contacted me on this subject have spent literally tens of thousands of dollars on surgery and health care trying to keep their pets here on earth with them. Some, like this author, have traveled great distances to meet with specialists. Many have sat up all night, night after night, providing comfort and care for ailing and aging pets.

There can be little doubt but that people who love their pets—people just like you—will exhaust every possibility to help them. No expense, no inconvenience, no commitment will be too much. Sadly, however, despite all of your selfless efforts and expense, your best friend will likely continue to deteriorate, often in great pain.

You are then forced to make that dreaded big decision, whether or not to let your little buddy go. It is a most difficult decision-making process, and often we procrastinate until we are faced with no choice at all and are motivated by the intense suffering and pain our pet is enduring. What makes this situation even harder is that, commonly, our pets will hold on without complaint for as long as we want them to.

As painful of a process as all of this is, it isn't until after the decision has been made and our best friend is gone, that the real pain begins. Almost without exception, guilt comes, accompanied by its infamous associate, doubt. Together they rob us of our confidence, and we begin to wonder whether we did the right thing. We second-guess our decision and beat ourselves up in our hearts and minds, allowing questions to haunt us, like: *Did I do the right thing? Should I have waited longer?* Or, *What if I had done this or that?*

No one, me included, is in the position to presumptuously determine that putting your best friend down was the right thing for you to do. Even veterinarians can get it wrong. Sometimes the prognosis is right-on, but often their advice amounts to nothing more than a guess. Ultimately, you have to make the decision, basing it upon all the factors available to you at the time.

No one can tell you when it is the right time, and no one should ever second-guess you after the fact by saying that it was the wrong time. We just cannot know. We make the best decision we can based on what we feel is the right thing to do.

If you ask me, as many readers have, I could never tell you whether the decision was made too soon, whether it was made too late, or whether it should have been made at all. At best, my thoughts in those areas would be nothing more than a subjective guess, based upon very limited information and my own values and level of sensitivity.

It would be unfair to hold everyone to my own personal criteria and to respond to them based upon that alone. Instead, what I can do is encourage you to remember how things were at that moment in time when you bore the responsibility of making that big decision. Only you can know whether it was the right and timely thing to do. My advice to you is to simply *"trust the moment."*

By that, I mean that you should not second-guess now the decision that you made then, when strength was needed. Second-guessing will only lead to a feeling of insecurity, which will eventually manifest itself as guilt. It is imperative to trust that at that moment, when you were forced to make that undesirable big decision, you absolutely did so from a position of love.

You didn't want to do it. It horrified you to have to decide. Nevertheless, you stepped up and assumed the responsibility you had assumed when you took a pet into your home. You selflessly decided, at that moment, that your best friend was suffering and that there was nothing you or anyone else could do about it, except for you to make that decision.

Now, long after the fact, divorced from the intense emotion and the pressure of that moment, you are allowing yourself to dissect and analyze every thought and circumstance. Now, with the luxury of time, you are starting to rethink the facts and question yourself, playing the "what if" game. Today, it isn't as clear as it was then. You wonder whether the pain and suffering your pet was enduring was really that bad after all. You really don't know whether you did the right thing.

Take heart—it is human nature to doubt. We are imperfect and fickle creatures. But that does not make it right to put a load of guilt upon ourselves. Second-guessing does not change the reality of the moment when you had to make that big decision. Don't let your feelings of grief give birth to guilt. Remember the moment. Remember that, at that moment, you wanted nothing more than to help the one you so dearly loved. You would have done anything, paid any amount, performed any feat, to prolong their life, but it was just not to be.

The doctor's prognosis was grim. There would be much suffering and pain. The recommendation was to bring them relief, to help them pass on. Under extreme duress and emotional strain, through tears of love, you weighed all the facts, reached down deep inside yourself, put aside your own selfish desire to have your pet hang on and stay here with you, and you did what you thought was best for them at that moment.

At that moment, your love made the selfless decision that rationality and logic now question. There was no selfishness then, but rather a somber consideration of the facts, and a decision to do something that you really did not want to do. But you did it, because someone else—your best friend—needed for you to be strong for them. You put self aside and found strength you did not know that you had in order to be unselfish and put their relief from suffering above your own desires.

Never let go of that moment. Hold on to it. Trust it. Trust that you were right and that you did what was needed. Trust that your love ruled over your selfishness, and know that where your love prevailed, there is no room for guilt or doubt. Grief and sadness are important validations of your love, but do not cheat that process with doubt, regret, and guilt. Guilt has no place where love has demonstrated itself.

Here is a tool that I recommend to readers who contact me

who are yet considering putting their pet down. If you can muster the strength and wherewithal to do this, literally hours before you take your pet to the veterinarian, write yourself a letter explaining why you have decided to proceed. Be explicit and list every feeling and thought you have. Make sure you capture every reason you feel it is the right time. Undoubtedly, the paper will be stained with your tears, but try to force yourself to do this. And then tuck that letter away in a dresser drawer somewhere.

Later, when the second-guessing starts (and it will start), find that letter and read it. It will remind you of why you had no other choice, and it will subdue and hopefully slay the feelings of guilt. Grief is enough of a burden without adding guilt and regret to it.

I hope that the information I've provided in this chapter is never needed. If it is, I hope it helps to ease the stress and grief that people experience when they must put an animal to sleep. If you have additional questions, you have my e-mail address. I answer all mail personally and promptly. Sometimes it gets a little overwhelming, but I will respond just as quickly as I can.

Let us move on now to the other half of people who contact me with questions about euthanasia. These would be those who have not yet made the decision, but who are looking for help in making that decision. The questions I usually get from this group of pet lovers include, but are not limited to:

- When will I know it is time to let him/her go?
- Do you think God will be mad at me for doing this?
- How do I explain this to my children?

To the first two questions, I have to again say that this puts me in a very difficult and awkward situation. With the limited information that I am provided from most letters and e-mails, I could never make a determination as to when the time would be right for someone to euthanize their pet. And not knowing the religious beliefs of the person contacting me, I would run the risk of offending them with an answer fit for my own personal faith.

But they are looking for a quick response, and I feel obligated to give them the best answers that I can, considering the circumstances. Undoubtedly, some reading this will one day find themselves as part of this group, if you are not so now, so it behooves me to give you some guidance here.

On the first question, it has been my experience that pets are like children when it comes to illness. The signals are fairly obvious. They can become lethargic, stop eating, sleep too much or too little, have sensitivity to the touch in certain areas (i.e., the appendix in children, the joints in animals, etc.), and they are basically just not their same old selves.

Like with our own children, we become concerned and rush them off for the appropriate medical evaluation. When the diagnosis and prognosis are grim, we gain as much knowledge about their condition and what to expect, load up on any medications that will ease their suffering, and become vigilant in their care.

Armed with knowledge about whatever terminal illness ails them, we can decide early what signs to watch for that signal that their time of passing is near. And when that time comes, or if their suffering becomes unbearable, we will know that the time is right.

On the second question, I feel tempted to take the coward's way out and say that readers need to default to their own faith and beliefs for an answer to this. But I won't; this book is meant to help, and dodging questions does not fit into that blueprint. Nevertheless, I do have to say that my view will be strictly Christian and biblical. Even that does not afford me a safe haven, as there are such a variety of beliefs that gather under that banner.

So I will be direct and succinct in my response to this question. Euthanasia is not a biblical teaching. In my opinion, it is almost akin to human sacrifice, which is frowned upon in the Scriptures. But those tenets apply to human beings. With animals, there comes a greater responsibility to the caretaker.

God charges us with the proper care and oversight of animals. I think there is room for a lot of subjective thought in this matter. I would not try to argue down someone's point of view if they were against euthanizing animals. Similarly, I would not try to argue down someone's point of view if they were for it.

It truly is a matter not directly addressed in the Scriptures, and instead it is left up to personal conviction and understanding. Obviously, by my own admission, I have helped several of my own animals to pass. But each time it was when there was absolutely no hope and their frail bodies couldn't possibly stand to endure any more suffering. In fact—may they forgive me—I think that several times I selfishly waited too long, not wanting to give them up.

One should evaluate the dictates of their own heart, their convictions of faith, and the needs of the animal under their charge in order to come to the right decision for them on this matter.

And finally, the third commonly asked question in this section: how to explain euthanasia to our children. I will defer this answer to the section "What to Share with Your Child" below.

What to Share with Your Child

Talking with a child about the unexpected death of a pet is tough enough, but explaining to them that their living pet will not be with them much longer is on an entirely different scale of difficulty. This is an undertaking that you need to plan and prepare well for. I recommend that you do not limit yourself to what I write here, but seek out other professional guidance, as well.

There are myriad books available that deal with the bereavement of children in general, and also those that target specific age-groups, specifically how they view the world and interpret news like this. They are written by professionals who specialize in dealing with bereaved children, and they are quite conscientious. I know because I have corresponded with some of the psychologists who wrote them. Several have contacted me and asked (and received) my permission to use some of my material in their books and as part of the grief support regimen that they use in their clinics.

My short presentation for you to use with your child will not be anything like what those books offer. Decades ago, I took time to skim through some of the secular books that addressed bereaved children. The few things I read made me very sad. I don't mean that they were poorly written. They were not. In fact, the authors were quite articulate and documented well their findings and suggestions. From a clinical point of view, they were excellent works.

It was the subliminal message they sent that bothered me. They spoke about explaining to children that death was absolutely permanent, in the sense that once a person (or animal) was gone, that was it: kaput, over, *fin*. There was no other life or hope for them. Whether intentionally or unintentionally I do not know, but invariably, they ignored any direct reference to faith in God and spiritual matters.

They did encourage readers to seek out spiritual help from ministers of their respective faiths, which is a good thing, I suppose. But that recommendation seemed to be undermined by their personal disbelief in God, which they were not ashamed to express to readers. Essentially, I found them to be disingenuous when it came to suggesting that readers seek spiritual counseling.

Another common thread that ran through all the books that I read was their constant encouragement to seek closure. I had to read and reread those entries to understand what they were saying. And what they meant that was that, since we knew there was nothing further beyond this life, we should be able to move on and close this chapter of ours and our pet's life. Okay, there was more to it than that, but that part of it stood out to me and was far from my liking.

However, the purpose of this book is not to nitpick the words of other authors with differing views. It is to provide encouragement and help for people who have had to euthanize a beloved pet. I only mentioned those secular works so that you would know that I take a much different path in providing encouragement. God has not been expelled from this book.

In fact, this chapter—indeed, this whole book—allows God to weigh in on the weightier matters of death and all it entails. My objective is to give hope, not bring closure. I don't want to forget my departed pets and move on. I want to remember them and look forward to the day when I shall see them again. I may be wrong, but I think you want that, too—for you and for your children.

If I understand the Bible correctly, and I assure you I do, physical death is not the end. It is not the "closure" of a life. It is merely a doorway to the next life. Now, admittedly, humans have some decisions to make in their relationship with God to determine to where that doorway leads, but animals do not. They are innocent creatures, and their eternity is already sealed and sure. And this is the hope that I want to convey to children (and their parents), not some faithless, defeatist closure mumbo jumbo.

Turning now to our objective in this chapter, I think you know that you are probably going to face at least two very difficult moments. Your initial talk with your children, when you share with them the bad news, is going to be very difficult. There will be many tears and many questions.

Most children will react this way, but do not be surprised if your child does not react in this way. Some children show no reaction initially, but that does not mean they are not hurt deeply and starting the grieving process. Keep being vigilant with that child, as they will probably break down in sorrow eventually.

Then there will be the actual day when you will be euthanizing your pet. This will probably prove to be the most difficult time. Initially, it hurt your children to learn the news, but since the pet was still there in the home, regardless of its medical condition, the news of the impending death probably was less "real" for them.

Now, with the day upon them, reality will set in and all the pain will come flooding to the surface again, but this time in much greater force. This is not true with just children; you also will feel the resurgence of grief.

Without further delay, let me provide a suggested script for you to use with your children for that initial meeting. It is a very simple offering, but it needs to be simple for children. They need for you to be clear and to the point. The better they understand, the easier it will be for them to grasp and accept the news.

As usual, I would expect that you would adapt what I say to accommodate your personal situation and circumstances. I would also suggest that when the day comes to bid farewell to your pet, you simply reuse the following in whatever form fits the situation.

SCRIPT: "PREPARING YOUR CHILD FOR THE LOSS OF A PET"

Children, your father (mother) and I have something very important to talk to you about. It is very sad news, I am afraid, and I am so sorry to have to tell it to you. It is about Buddy. He is okay right now, but he is very sick.

You know that we have taken him to the veterinarian, Dr. Smith, many times in the last couple of weeks. I know that he seemed like he might be getting better, but we were told today that he isn't.

Buddy is very old, and his body is not working as well as it used to. You know how sometimes he is not able even to get up anymore. We have to help him. And then it is painful for him to stand or walk.

He is always in so much pain. You know how some of the older people at church use canes and wheelchairs to help them walk? That is because their bodies have gotten old and do not work as well as they used to. Buddy is like that now. He has grown old like them, but he can't use a cane or a wheelchair to help with the pain. So, when he tries to get up and walk, it hurts him a lot. And we don't want him to hurt, do we?

Dr. Smith has told us that over the next few weeks, Buddy's pain is going to get even worse and he won't be able to stand up or walk at all. You know how sometimes he has bad days and he just stays in his bed and cries a little. Even when he is lying down, the pain sometimes makes him cry.

Dr. Smith told your dad and me that if we really loved Buddy, we should help end his pain for him, because he can't help himself. What he meant was that we should stop giving him the medication he is taking and let him go.

I know that makes you very sad. It makes Dad and me very sad, too. We don't want to see Buddy die, but it seems like that is the only way to make the pain stop for him. I think if Buddy could talk to us right now, he would tell us that he needs for the pain to stop. It is getting to be too much for him. And we want to do what Buddy would want and need, don't we?

Buddy needs for us to be strong to help him. He helped us whenever we needed him. Remember the time when we had coyotes in the yard and Buddy barked and scared them away? Or the time when he jumped on that spider that came in the house? He knew we needed his help, and he was there for us. And now he needs our help and we need to be there for him. We need to help him end his pain.

I know death seems scary to you, but sometimes we let death be scarier than it really is. We know from the Bible that God has a wonderful place called heaven, where people and animals go after they die. That is where Buddy will go if we help him to go there.

In heaven we know that people and animals are made young again, and all the pain and sickness they had back here is gone and will never come back. If we let Buddy go to heaven, his pain will stop and he will be able to stand and run again. He won't need medication. He won't need us to help him stand up. He will be so happy to feel good again.

And someday we will see Buddy again. Death does not mean the end. It is a new beginning, a very nice new beginning. You know when we go to the zoo, the animals there all want to get away and leave. And at the circus, the animals there want to leave, too. But no animals want to leave heaven. It is too wonderful of a place to leave. So, Buddy won't leave there, but we will see him when we get there ourselves one day.

Now, I know it will be hard to let Buddy go, but if we think about how good this new life will be for him, it should help us to smile for him. Yes, we will be a little unhappy, but we are going to help each other get through the sadness. We are going to meet together each day just like this to pray and talk about God's promises in the Bible and how He is taking care of Buddy.

We will call our time each day "Daily Devotions," and I am sure it will be a nice time when we can learn more and believe more that God is taking care of Buddy and all the rest of His animals. Remember the story of the ark and Noah? God was so concerned about His animals that He had Noah build an ark to carry them safely through the flood.

God hasn't changed. He will not lose any of His animals. He still loves them all, including Buddy, because they belong to Him. We may think Buddy is ours, but he really belongs to God. God lent him to us because He knew we would love him and take care of him and help him when he got old. And we have, and God is very happy that we did that.

God knew that when Buddy got old and would be in a lot of pain, we would send him back to Him so He could take care of him. God will show Buddy such love when he gets there.

I am sorry we had to bring this bad news to you, but I hope you see how important it is that we help Buddy now. We have to be brave and strong, because it is hard for us to do this for Buddy, but we have to help him. We have to think about him first and not ourselves.

We have some time now to spend with Buddy and to show him how much we love him. That will make him very happy. And we will help each other, too, not just when we have our evening devotions, but all day, every day. We will show our love for Buddy by our love for each other. He will be so happy to know that we are okay because we know that he is okay.

Chapter 13

THE RAINBOW BRIDGE

Anyone who has grieved the loss of a beloved pet and who has access to a computer has probably read, or at least heard of, the poem "The Rainbow Bridge." This poem, or at least one of the many versions of it, can be found on literally hundreds of genre-specific and social media websites, and even in chat rooms that deal with pet loss and bereavement.

This anonymous poem speaks of a bridge in heaven where pets sit patiently waiting for their people to arrive. It is a touching piece of prose that soothes the grieving heart and captures the hopes of those who have lost a beloved family pet and best friend.

Several hundred thoughtful readers have shared copies of this poem with me over the years. I think at last count I identified nine variations in the poem among the many copies sent to me. Apparently there are other anonymous folks out there who feel they could improve upon the original. Whatever version I have received, I appreciated the thoughtfulness of these kindhearted folks for taking time out of their busy days to share the poem with me.

But often, those who send me copies have questions about the poem that they want answered, and for some reason they feel I would have those answers. The questions are usually the same:

- 🐾 What do you think of the poem?
- 🐾 Is it true?
- 🐾 Is it accurate?
- 🐾 Is there such a bridge mentioned in the Bible?
- 🐾 Will my best friend be there waiting for me?

People often ask me if I am the anonymous author of "The Rainbow Bridge."

Less often, but enough times to be very flattering, I have been asked if I was the anonymous author of this touching poem. Some even observed that the verbal flair that I use in writing my books was evident in the poem.

I would like to share my answers to these questions here as a help for you and your children. I may not necessarily answer the questions in the same order I placed them above, but I will address each concern.

To begin, I want to be clear on my response to the suspicion that I am the author of "The Rainbow Bridge." I definitely am not. I am not being humble, as some have supposed, nor do I write anything as a ghost author or use another pen name to write.

I do not agree that my personal flair is reflected in this poem.

In fact, I am not really sure that I even have a personal flair. The poem may reflect, as some have pointed out, the same compassion that readers find in my books, but I assure you, this poem is not my work.

My research shows that the poem was first published somewhere in the mid- to late-1980s. I did not author my first book, *Cold Noses at the Pearly Gates*, until 1996. Previous to that, the only real writing I did was for technical publications for the United States Coast Guard and an article for *Proceedings*, a magazine published by the United States Naval Institute.

I do not mean to seem ungracious or ungrateful. I am genuinely flattered that some appreciate my work and thought I might have authored the poem, but it was not me. And I want to put that misconception to rest once and for all.

To help me answer the other questions about the bridge and whether our pets are waiting there for us, I thought it would be a good idea to post here the original poem for your convenience and quick reference. Unfortunately, as I acknowledged earlier, there are several versions floating around the Internet, and determining which version was the original proved to be an arduous and impossible task.

However, this tidbit of information might interest you. I actually found it quite humorous. I discovered that, although the poem is widely accepted to be anonymous, almost all of the versions I located had copyrights attached to them, with strict warnings against reproduction. Ironically, it appears that even the true author would not be allowed to make copies of his or her own work if they were inclined to obtain a copy.

Though I could not determine which version was the original, all is not lost. Here is the version that seems to be most wide-spread on the Internet than all the others combined. Coinciden-tally, it is also the version that readers send to me most frequently. And, thankfully, it is not encumbered with the same copyright warnings attached to the others.

The fact that it always appears with "Author Unknown" at the bottom suggests to me that it may, indeed, be the original, but, of course, we cannot be sure. In any event, this version cap-tures the essence of all the other versions and will serve our pur-poses here.

The Rainbow Bridge

Just this side of heaven is a place called the Rainbow Bridge. When an animal dies that has been especially close to someone here, that pet goes to the Rainbow Bridge. There are meadows and hills for all of our special friends, so they can run and play together. There is plenty of food, water, and sunshine, and our friends are warm and comfortable.

All the animals who had been ill and old are restored to health and vigor; those who were hurt or maimed are made whole and strong again, just as we remember them in our dreams of days and times gone by. The animals are happy and content, except for one small thing: They each miss someone very special to them, who had to be left behind.

They all run and play together, but the day comes
when one suddenly stops and looks into the
distance. His bright eyes are intent; his eager body
quivers. Suddenly he begins to run from the group,
flying over the green grass, his legs carrying him
faster and faster.
You have been spotted, and when you and your
special friend finally meet, you cling together in
joyous reunion, never to be parted again. The
happy kisses rain upon your face; your hands
again caress the beloved head, and you look
once more into the trusting eyes of your pet,
so long gone from your life but never absent
from your heart. Then you cross the Rainbow
Bridge together. . . .

—Author Unknown

Regarding the origins of the poem, my best guess is that it was authored by someone who had lost a dear and cherished pet. Quite likely, perhaps even obviously, that person was acquainted with Norse legends and folklore, in particular, the legend of Bifrost. Attempting to console themselves, they adapted that Norse legend to include animals, and specifically family pets.

Bifrost, in Norse mythology, is the bridge between the realm of mankind, called Midgard, and the realm of the Norse gods, Asgard. The bridge is described differently in various writings, but generally the bridge is said to be encased in some sort of supernatural flame and is comprised of many colors, which is where the rainbow reference apparently comes from.

Though it has no bearing on this study, it is interesting to note that the remains of exceedingly large humanoids found around the world are often connected to this same legend. The bones, usually of individuals eight feet tall or greater, are alleged to be those of ancient Vikings or Norsemen. Apparently, according to the legend, the mythical bridge was used by giants to enter this world.

Of course, I cannot be sure of my assumption that the poem about the Rainbow Bridge came about as a result of someone with knowledge of this legend applying the myth to their own needs concerning animals. But that is not really a concern for me, as you will see with my answer to the other questions. It was just some peripheral information that I thought you might find interesting.

In regard to the questions I have been asked, I can say without hesitation or reservation that the Rainbow Bridge is not real. It is simply a myth, Norse or not. It is definitely not mentioned in the Bible, and it is not a part of the heaven of the Bible. That is my quick answer, and I know it will not sit well with everyone. But my hope is that you will read my more considered response in the following. I am sure you will find my reasoning lucid and convincing. Hopefully, it will also be comforting.

While I will admit that the poem is pleasant and generally very comforting, that it has no doubt helped many an ailing heart, it simply is not biblical. One of the most critical elements of the Christian hope is that God promised that heaven will be nothing like earth. All the pain and suffering, death and sorrow, unfairness and injustice—those things of earth will not be present or found in heaven.

It is inconceivable, then, that our animals could sit sadly waiting for our arrival. What a pitiful scene it would be to see such sorrow and longing right at heaven's door. If they could be sad, what would be the difference of this place from earth? What would be the reason to go there, if things there were the same as here? The most potent, persuasive, and promising thing about heaven is that it will be a place of bliss without regret, pining, or sadness.

And let us graduate this thought and bring it to full fruition. What would happen to these hapless creatures waiting on this bridge if their people did *not* make it to heaven? Oh my, that is one eventuality that the poet did not take into consideration. Would they just remain there, suffering in loneliness forever? Would they slink away into some corner of heaven to grieve for all eternity? Doesn't sound like much of a heaven to me.

And the fact that the bridge is not biblical is not my only objection; there is another failing in this poem. It also makes the assumption that the animals that have passed continue to belong to us. I have made this assumption myself with just about every pet the Lord has entrusted to my care.

The truth is, that while a special bond will undoubtedly forever exist with the animals with whom we shared our lives, there can be no doubt but that they belong to their Creator, God. We are given temporary dominion over them and are charged with caring for them. We develop relationships with them that will last for eternity. But ultimately and rightfully, they belong to their Creator.

Again, I do not dislike the poem. I know it has helped many. It helped me; I wept as I read the words, because they stirred the hope I held that somehow, someway, I would see my precious friends again.

It deserves credit for at least that. But when it comes to eternity, only the Bible can offer insight that we can trust and in which we can place our confidence, not some anonymous piece of poetry.

If I were to author a poem to capture the promises of God and the reality of heaven, it would be biblically based, such as the following. (Please note, the reference to "man" here means "mankind.")

Reunion Meadow

In innocence you were formed, a loving
and living soul.
Entrusted to man's care, your presence
made him whole,
By his error, and not your own, you suffered
from his fall.
His fate became your own, as death doth
claim us all.

No matter that result, you lived your life for man.
A noble, devoted creature, alongside him
you ever ran.
You cared for his flocks, protected his
family and home,
Licked his hand in love, rewarded with
just a bone.

Or purred warmly for the one who opened
heart and home,
Who gave you love and shelter so you would
need not roam,
Never turning on the hand you loved, never aware
of life above,
Giving your all to the one you served, and doing
so with love.

Passing from their blessed care, you will
be greatly missed,
But the Creator promises we will meet again, we
can trust in this.
In that place of promise, far from here
on heaven's shore,
Lies a meadow of peace and reunion, where we
shall meet once more.

—Gary Kurz

I hope that learning that the "Rainbow Bridge" poem is not only anonymous, but fictitious, will not cause you any despair or discomfort. The promises of God regarding the animals that He created and loves are so much more potent and sweet, in terms of their eternal welfare.

On the fabled bridge they would pine away for who knows how long, waiting on their special person to show up. For some whose person would never show, their despair would be grievously unbearable. How could this be considered a place of happiness and rest? But in the hands of the Almighty, they would

neither pine nor despair. They would enjoy immediate whole-
ness and happiness.

That happiness would be increased exponentially when their
person or people arrived, but it would not wane at all if they did
not. Heaven is a place of bliss and happiness, and nothing like
this life we will leave behind. Regardless, the point is that they
will be happy in any circumstance and not sitting unfulfilled and
unhappy on some mythical bridge.

What to Share with Your Child

This chapter was provided for the edification of parents,
specifically to clarify the biblical position on eternity and the re-
union(s) to which we all look forward. I would not share this information with children unless they specifically ask about the
Rainbow Bridge. I would then share the poem "Reunion Meadow" with them instead.

If they have already read "The Rainbow Bridge" and have
questions about it, I would suggest you refrain from discussing
Norse mythology and simply explain that you do not think the
whole poem is true, because it hurts to think our animals would
be pining away awaiting our arrival, or something along those
lines.

Chapter 14

HELPING THE FAMILY HEAL

Few of us are prepared for the trauma that comes with the loss of the beloved family pet. Unless we have previously endured other such losses, we are completely blindsided by the impact this life experience has upon us and our family.

If the loss is an anticipated passing, due to age or illness of the pet, we may be able to prepare ourselves mentally beforehand to avoid the shock that comes with losing them unexpectedly. But no amount of preparation can lessen our emotional reaction to losing someone we love.

And the tenure of the pet has little to do with the level of shock and grief we feel when they are suddenly taken from us. People who love animals bond very quickly and very deeply with them; a one-year bond is as strong as a ten-year relationship. Admittedly, there are more memories associated with a longer relationship, but memories only sweeten the bond, not make it stronger.

If the family is closely knit together with the pet, the probability is that all will feel the loss equally and grieve accordingly. Some may deal with their grief differently than other family members, perhaps even privately so that their grief is not obvious to others. But commonly, all will feel a sense of great loss accompanied by intense sorrow.

That grief will manifest itself in individual ways, but inevitably, each member of the family will experience the many stages of grief that professional counselors warn us about. It is not my purpose here to discuss the grieving process or the various stages of grief that one might experience. There are many books available for that purpose, and if you feel that professional help is needed, for either yourself or your child, I recommend strongly that you seek out that help.

I am merely offering parents answers to questions that are commonly asked by children, questions that tens of thousands of readers have asked me over a period of twenty years on behalf of their children. For them, and for you, I bring to focus my experience as a pet loss author, my biblical education and knowledge, my understanding of God's providence for His animals, and my own love for animals and for people.

And it has been my experience, through lengthy exchanges with those many readers, that grief is more than just a clinical process. Potentially, it evolves into a long-term emotional condition with which we must live. That condition is called sorrow. Sorrow has a much greater longevity than grief. In fact, it is likely that we are never really free from it. Even the Lord was referred to in the Scriptures as "a man of sorrows, and acquainted with grief" (Isaiah 53:3).

Presumably, adults will handle this sorrow better than children, because it is not new to them. Most, if not all, adults have previously experienced sorrow and have learned how to live a normal existence with it. They are familiar with the mood swings caused by memories and have learned how to compartmentalize their feelings and accommodate those "down" moments. Many have also identified the "triggers" for their sorrow and know how to avoid them.

Sorrow can be triggered at any time and in any place, and it usually comes upon us without warning. Sights, sounds, even odors can be triggers for sorrow. Any stimulus that stirs a memory that you associate with the family pet can be a trigger that brings sorrow to the surface of your consciousness.

If sorrow is triggered when you are alone and at your leisure, it poses little inconvenience, and you may indulge yourself and weep. It is common knowledge that weeping is an excellent way to vent and help the "sting" of sorrow subside. But if you find yourself in a social setting, such as at work or in a meeting, where it is imperative that you maintain your professional composure, sorrow can be a very unsettling and embarrassing thing to deal with.

There are many mental tricks or exercises that we can perform to help us neutralize those triggers. It takes a little effort and a little more willpower, but you can keep sorrow at bay when you need to—at least temporarily.

The trick is simple. When you trip one of the triggers that bring on sorrowful memories, immediately force yourself to think of something else. It can be any number of things, from working an algebraic formula in your head (or on paper if you must) to thinking about a romantic night you had with your husband or wife.

My personal "go to" exercise is to think about building something. I happen to like building sheds. So, when I find myself remembering precious moments, at the first twinge of sorrow, I force my mind to think about building a shed. I plan what size of shed I want, what materials I will need, and how much it will cost.

I spend about three or four minutes in that exercise, and that is about all the time it takes to have successfully diverted my mind from sorrow to something more productive. I actually followed through on one of my designs and built a very nice shed. Thankfully, I have not followed through each time I use that exercise or I would have one hundred sheds in my backyard.

But the point is that this works. It is a tool, or a strategy, that you can use, not only for yourself, but for your children. Obviously, you won't be planning the building of a shed with a child. But there are myriad things that you can use to divert their attention away from the pain they are feeling.

You might ask them to read you a story out of one of their books, or ask them to name all of the other children in their class at school, for instance. Asking them to tell you about one of their hobbies would be another way to divert their attention.

The key here is to "preplan." When your child is feeling low, have something ready: a story, a joke, a surprise present, or anything else that will guide their attention away from the pain. Sorrow is an emotional response to thoughts and memories. Displace those painful thoughts and memories with other mental stimuli.

Adults not only have the advantage of having experienced sorrow previously, and therefore an understanding of how to cope with it, but they also know from those experiences that in time, the pain will pass and things will get better for them. The old cliché is anchored in truth: Time does heal all things.

I can use myself as an example. While I am certain that the sorrow for my departed pets will be with me for the duration of my life, I no longer have bouts of sorrow to the level that I have to think about building sheds. Time may not have completely healed, but it has greatly helped.

Unfortunately, children are not equipped for handling grief or sorrow like an adult. Children have very few life experiences to rely on to help them maintain emotional balance and stability. They are innocent, and for the most part, they have been protected from the evils of the world by you, their loving parent or guardian.

In their innocent eyes, the traumatic event of losing their "best friend" can seem like the end of the world, especially if they have that special bond that most children have with the family pet. The pain can seem insurmountable for them, and their only hope of finding relief from their sorrow is if Mom and Dad rally to help them.

Parents need to be proactive when it comes to helping their children through the trauma of losing their pet. I am sure that you are being proactive in this way, or you wouldn't be earnestly seeking ways to help, like reading this book. I have tried to help you by giving you dependable, time-tested, Bible-based answers to the questions children often ask. I have provided an analysis of the scriptures used and suggested presentations that I hope you have found helpful.

There are tricks we can teach ourselves to keep painful memories from hurting so much.

I would like to offer two additional suggestions, or tools, in the following paragraphs that I think might serve you well in your attempts to help your child cope with their recent loss. The first is only that—a suggestion. I emphasize that, because undoubtedly many of you will balk at my suggestion or perhaps totally ignore it. And I understand completely why you might reject it, given the current emotional state of your family.

But this suggestion could be a very useful tool for you and a great help to your child. I hope you will at least hear me out. Countless readers have reluctantly taken my advice over the years and invariably found it to be a sage strategy. I honestly could not tell you how many wonderful people have expressed their appreciation for my urging them to try this tactic.

And the suggestion is that you consider acquiring another pet. Now then, I am not trying to give credence to the callous friends who flippantly say to you in your hour of pain, "Oh, it was just a cat. Get another one." Far from it! What I am saying is that a new pet can be a balm to the hearts of children; indeed, to the whole family.

Adults have a difficult time accepting the idea of acquiring a new pet so soon after the passing of their beloved best friend. Somehow we feel we are betraying the memory of the one who has passed on ahead, that we are replacing them. But nothing could be further from the truth. That place in our heart that held Buddy in love will always belong to Buddy. But I have found that people who love pets have *huge* hearts, and there is always room for another pet to be loved—in fact, several others.

Rather than view this as a betrayal, consider it a tribute to the one who has gone on ahead. What an honor for you to rescue one of their own, honoring their memory in that way!

And please consider this: Animals in a pet store do not need to be rescued. If you do not take one home, it is almost guaranteed that someone else will. Animals in pet stores are not in danger like those in shelters and animal control facilities. If you visit one of those places, you will find that the animals there are just as cute and just as loving as in any pet store. They will melt your heart just as quickly and thoroughly.

And the out-of-pocket cost to you will be so much less. I recently visited a pet store to see what kind of prices puppies and kittens were going for. I was shocked. One West Highland white terrier was priced at $1,600. Conversely, I have rescued three in the recent past; one from a shelter in Galveston, Texas, and two others from puppy mills in Kansas.

The one in Texas was a day away from being destroyed, and the two in Kansas were scheduled to be put down due to slight "defects." They would never sell to a pet store, you see. In all, my expenses were approximately $300 for all three, which included their spaying.

One of the two I rescued from the puppy mill was a puppy that had a slight overbite, but she was beautiful. She turned out to be the most wonderful dog I ever had—and my shadow and my confidant. And these people were going to destroy her because she would not be profitable to them.

That aside, there are two points I want to make about these experiences. First, my cost for each of these pets was less than $50, and all of them were the sweetest, most loving companions. And second (and please don't laugh), they seemed to know that I was their only chance. They seemed to be waiting for someone to walk through the door, point them out, and say, "That one . . . that's the one." What a warm feeling of being needed and appreciated this brought to me.

But keep your eye on the prize. The real reward is not helping another animal find a home, although that is a wonderful thing. The real prize is the healing of your child's heart. If you lost a cherished dog, there is nothing like a warm and loving puppy to put a smile back on your child's face. If the family pet was a cat, how wonderful it would be to have a playful kitten entertaining the family once again. The pain will still be there, but the need to have and love a community pet will be satisfied, and that will pay big emotional dividends.

I understand that this strategy—and I really hate to call it that, because it sounds rather cold—is not for everyone. Some folks just are not ready and won't be for some time. You must be true to yourself and your family in this matter. If you feel it is too soon and you do not find yourself wavering after reading my explanation, then you probably need to wait. But if you are straddling the fence, I can tell you that many have been there before you and taken my advice, and I haven't gotten a single complaint yet.

The second suggestion that I want to offer to you, I think you will find much more palatable. I have put together seven days of devotionals that I hope will help your child understand and accept the passing of their pet more easily. Each day's devotional will be presented in the following chapters for your convenience.

If you are not familiar with what a devotional is, it is simply a short reflection on a truth from the Word of God that, in this case, is aimed at helping the family heal from the trauma of the loss of a beloved pet. At the end of this chapter, I provide you with a suggested matrix/format to follow to assist you.

I will attempt to write each of the seven devotionals at the interest level of six- to twelve-year-olds. Please forgive me if your child is younger or older than this. I feel that the majority of children for whom you are seeking help will be in the age-group I have selected, and so I will try to confine myself to writing to them. I trust you will be able to adjust the devotionals to your child's age.

Also, please keep in mind that today's six- to twelve-year-olds are a whole lot smarter than we were at their age. Technology has given them learning tools that we never had access to. It presents a challenge to me, and to you, to try to meet them at their level. But hopefully, working together, we will be successful.

Finally, I will be using stories and applications that may not fit precisely to your situation, or that might not work perfectly for your family. Most of the stories I use will be actual accounts of something that happened, but occasionally I may use a made-up story to emphasize a point for them. You may have to adapt those stories so they work for you and your child. My examples and memories may not mean as much to them as something they can relate to from their own past.

As promised, the following is a suggested format that you may want to employ as you present the day's devotion to your family each evening. My wife and I used this format for years with our children. It gave us an organized way to help shape their values and morals, strengthen their beliefs, bond us closer as a family, and address the problems they faced in life. You may not want to use the same format, but so you have some idea of how devotionals work, this is how our ten- to twelve-minute sessions went:

- We would meet each evening at the same time.
- Each member would share with the family how their day went, especially any problems or accomplishments.
- We would spend a few minutes praising their accomplishments and praying for help with problems.
- I would share a short passage from the Scriptures and spend no more than five minutes expounding on what it said in a way that applied to us as a family.
- We would close with a short prayer (each day one family member would pray out loud for everyone's needs).

The devotionals that we will be using to help your family will be derived from **Galatians 5:22**, which says:

> *But the fruit of the Spirit is love, joy, peace, long-suffering, gentleness, goodness, faith. . . .*

I will be using each of the seven elements of the Holy Spirit's fruit consecutively in the seven daily devotions. The format will be similar to the format I have used in previous chapters. I will identify the devotional topic for that day, provide scriptural references and adult-level analysis, and then follow with a suggested short narrative to share with children at their level. Everything in the narrative in *italics* is intended for your use. Special notes intended just for parents are set in regular roman type.

Let us begin. Please move on to the next chapter.

Chapter 15

DAY 1 DEVOTIONAL: LOVE

The first element of the fruit of the Holy Spirit is *love*.

> *But the fruit of the Spirit is love, joy, peace, long-suffering, gentleness, goodness, faith. . . .*
>
> *—Galatians 5:22*

God's Word is primarily the revelation of His Son, the Lord Jesus Christ, to mankind, but it is also affectionately known as God's "love letter" to us. As such, there are innumerable passages we could turn to that highlight His love for us. But one that I find very applicable to this first day of devotion is **1 John 4:10**, which says:

> *Herein is love, not that we loved God, but that he loved us, and sent his Son to be the propitiation for our sins.*

Love is the predominant theme throughout the Bible. If God did not love us, there would be little need for Him to reach out to us as He does through His holy Word. That fact, in and of itself, is very comforting.

It is important to note that the Scriptures tell us that God loved us first. He didn't love us because we loved Him, which is usually the basis for healthy human relationships. Knowing our sinful ways and our penchant for wandering away from Him, He still loved us.

There are different kinds of love mentioned in the Bible. They are *agape*, or godly love; *eros*, or sensual love (as between a man and a woman); and *philos*, or brotherly love. God's *agape* love, explained in great detail in **1 Corinthians 13**, trumps all other considerations when it comes to His relationship with us. He simply loves us with an unmerited, but undying love. That love allowed His Son, the Lord Jesus Christ, to become the propitiation (or appeasement for God's wrath against sin) for us.

God loved us first!!!

As we face the calamities and traumas of this earthly life, we can sometimes forget that God loves us in a most perfect way. We erroneously assign blame for our problems and sorrow to Him. But the truth is, if God had His way, we would still be living in the peace and serenity of the Garden of Eden.

Adam and Eve chose to disobey, and as a result things changed to what we have today. Adam and Eve were not unique or any weaker than you or I. They acted as any of us would have acted. So the responsibility for the woes of this world is ours, not God's. One day, He will make all things right. Until then, we continue to exercise our free will and live with the ramifications that free will brings.

It is important, not only for our children, but also for us adults, to realize that God loves us. He loves us as much today as when the words to our text were penned nearly two thousand years ago. We often express our disappointments with what life throws at us with words like, "Why, God?" or, "Why did You let this happen to me, God?" But if we really believe that God loves us, and with a love more perfect than our own, logic would tell us that He would never do anything to actively bring us pain and sorrow.

When we lose a loved one—human or animal—we may automatically default to that carnal way of thinking and wonder why God allowed them to die. But the Scriptures suggest that God does not direct the death of a living being; He simply allows life to unfold. And unfortunately, death is now a part of the life process. The mortality rate is 100 percent, and it is that way as a result of sin in this world (**James 1:15**).

But God takes no pleasure in physical death. Again, if He had His way, there would be no end to our physical life. It grieves Him to see death. It grieves Him to see our sorrow. This is evidenced in the latter part of **John 11**, where Jesus had returned to the town of Bethany after receiving word that His friend Lazarus had passed away.

There, in verse 35, in two short but very potent words, we are given a glimpse of God's love for mankind. It simply says, "Jesus wept." He didn't weep because Lazarus was dead, because He knew that in a few moments He would raise His friend from death. But as He saw the sisters of Lazarus weeping and the Jews with them also weeping, we are told that "he groaned in his spirit and was troubled." The heart of God was broken for the people He had created. He never wanted them to suffer the ravages brought by sin. He saw their pain, He felt their sorrow, and it grieved Him to see them suffer.

That godly sentiment is expressed again in **Psalm 116:15**, as well. It says, "Precious in the sight of the LORD is the death of his saints." Now, admittedly this speaks of those who have placed their faith in God, and the application is that when a believer passes, it is a precious moment that does not escape the Lord's attention. But a preponderance of scriptures teaches us that no death escapes the ever-watchful eye of God and that all living things are of great importance to Him.

We refer to our pets as being "ours," but in truth they belong to their Creator and they are only on loan to us, husbandmen of His creatures, as it were. I address this in great detail in my book *Cold Noses at the Pearly Gates*, but briefly, the soul of every living creature is in God's hands. We forget that this life is the temporary one and that the next is the one that is permanent. When a living soul ends their finite life here, it begins its full and everlasting life there.

We mourn the loss of our cherished pets, and rightfully so. Their absence in our lives makes our road in life a little more difficult to travel. But we need to remember that God is love, and that He loves not only those He made in His image, but all of His creatures. When finite life ends here for our pets, infinite life begins for them there with God. There they are more than they were here, much more. Can we honestly mourn the changing of the caterpillar into a butterfly?

If you can convey these truths to your child, it will not take away their sorrow, but it will definitely take the edge off it. To know that the one we love is truly in a better place, that this is not just some canned cliché that people tell us to make us feel better, will resonate with the innocent heart of a child. It will most likely also fortify their faith in God.

What to Share with Your Child

Kids, this has been a very tough week for our family. It is important that we be together as a family, share each other's pain, and even cry together. So for the next week, your father and I (or your mother and I) want to meet together like this each evening for just a few minutes to try to encourage one another.

There is nothing wrong with allowing ourselves to weep. We all miss Buddy, and we all wish he could have stayed with us longer. But we should be happy that he lived a very long life and that his life was full of love. He was so happy to be part of this family, and he knew that you loved him as much as he loved you.

In the Bible, in 1 John 4:10, it says, "Herein is love, not that we loved God, but that he loved us. . . ." God loves all of us, but not only us; He loves the animals He created, too. The Bible is full of examples of how much God loves them.

Remember the story of Noah and the ark? God made the ark for Noah and his family, but He made Noah build it big enough so that thousands of animals would be safe on it, too. It took Noah over a hundred years to make that ark, but God waited because He wanted to keep His animals safe.

When Jesus was born, He was born in a stable among the animals. The people we see in the nativity scene came later. The shepherds came later that night, and the wise men, or the Magi, didn't come for almost two years. But the animals were there from the beginning, because they are important to God.

Then, when Jesus fasted in the wilderness for forty days, we are told that He spent His time among the wild animals. And there are so many other stories of how God loves all of His animals— the ones from long ago when Noah was alive, right up until today. If He didn't love our Buddy, He wouldn't have lent him to us to take such good care of him.

God says that the souls of all the animals are safe with Him, too. Right now, at this moment, Buddy is there in heaven with God. The life he had here with us was a good life, but his new life is so much better. There, in heaven, Buddy is able to communicate and understand better than he did here. And all the aches and pains he had back here in his old body are no more; now he is young again and able to run and jump like he used to do.

And the good thing about this new life is that it will never change. He will never grow old again. He will never have pain again. And one day, we will be able to be with him once more. And all of that is because God loves all those whom He created.

I think it would be good for all of us to remember out loud one memory that we have about Buddy and then tell the rest of the family one thing in heaven that you think might make Buddy happy. We will take turns. I will start . . .

One thing that I always remember about Buddy was his thumping tail. When he was lying on the wooden floor and someone would talk to him, he would wag his tail and it would thump, thump repeatedly on the floor and sound like someone was chopping a tree down outside. And the more we laughed at him, the more he thumped his tail. He was so funny.

As I think of him in heaven, right now, at this very moment, I think of how wonderful his life must be. When I think of Buddy trading in his old body for a new, younger one, I get the picture of a butterfly coming out of a cocoon. How wonderful and how beautiful life must be right now for our Buddy.

God loved us first.

Have each member of the family join in and contribute. Some may be reluctant, because they are not ready to articulate their pain. Give them a day or two; perhaps they will join in on another night. It probably is not wise to force them to participate. And never use guilt. Stick with just light encouragement.

The memories will undoubtedly draw tears, but sharing together as a family in this moment will strengthen each family member. Knowing that they are not alone in their pain will be of immense help in the healing process.

Remind your family each morning that you will be meeting again that evening and tell them what the topic will be so that they can be more prepared. Due to varying personal schedules, you might not be able to meet the same time each evening. In fact, prior commitments may preclude meeting every day. If you must skip a day, try to get back on track the following day. Bonding together and sharing memories and pain will go a long way toward the family returning to normal, both individually and collectively.

Chapter 16

DAY 2 DEVOTIONAL: JOY

The second element of the fruit of the Holy Spirit is *joy*.

> *But the fruit of the Spirit is love, joy, peace, long-suffering, gentleness, goodness, faith. . . .*
>
> —Galatians 5:22

We have all seen the T-shirts that people sport that carry slogans like I AM A WORK IN PROGRESS and GOD IS STILL WORKING ON ME. In truth, when someone accepts the Lord Jesus Christ as their Savior, they are, indeed, a work in progress. The Holy Spirit indwells them and begins the work of transforming them, or rather, conforming them to the image of Christ.

Previously, in this fifth chapter of Galatians, we are told what the works of our flesh are before we are indwelt by the Holy Spirit. Of the many things listed, none can be considered positive or productive.

So as the Spirit works from within to transform us and instill in us His fruit, we are eyewitnesses to and participants in our own spiritual growth. One day we will be able to sport a T-shirt that says WORK COMPLETE, but until then we endure the process of growth. And each step in that growth is a victory that helps us persevere over the works of the flesh. One in particular, joy, showcases how the fruit of the Spirit triumphs over the works of our flesh. I shall explain that statement in a moment.

I once listened to a comedian jest about the idiomatic misuse of words in the English language. With tongue in cheek, he spent about fifteen minutes offering some very witty examples. For instance, he pointed out that we call goods transported on the sea *CAR*go, but those same goods transported on land are called a *SHIP*ment.

He then asked the audience, "Why do we park in *DRIVE*-ways and drive on *PARK*ways?" He had them in stitches as he ran through a list of oxymoronic terms and misplaced words. He received an avalanche of laughs and a hearty round of applause as he cleverly pinged upon how we often use words in contrasting context.

Christians are not exempt from making similar vernacular mistakes when it comes to the language of the Bible. Sometimes we can inadvertently misuse words without even realizing it. For example, many use the words *soul* and *spirit* interchangeably in places where there is absolutely no similarity in their application. They are never used in the same way, nor do they ever mean the same thing.

Others hold erroneous views of what the word *wine* means, because they fail to realize that the same word is used for both alcoholic and nonalcoholic beverages in the Scriptures. Still oth-

ers confuse the words *Nazarite* and *Nazarene* when they speak
of the Lord Jesus Christ, wondering how He could raise people
from the dead when Nazarites were not permitted to be around
dead bodies. But, of course, He was not a Nazarite, but a Nazarene, which indicated what province He was from.

Admittedly, these types of "slips" are usually nothing more
than innocent miscues during casual conversations and no harm
is really caused to anyone. In fact, they can be quite humorous.
In any event, we understand what is meant and it is not necessary to champion corrections of every misuse of a biblical word
or term when we are merely conversing with each other.

There are times, however, when correction is warranted and
we should take a stand and speak up. Sometimes the misunderstanding of a word or words can adversely impact someone's personal Christian experience without their even knowing it. It is
the responsibility of a discerning brother or sister to help a younger
Christian understand more perfectly the components and bene-
fits of their faith.

A good example of this would be the commonly accepted use
of the two words *joy* and *happiness*. Like with the words *soul* and
spirit, we use them interchangeably without giving much thought
to whether they mean different things or not. But they do.

Because both words represent a positive state of mind, it is
easy to assume that both are similar in meaning. Who hasn't used
the phrase "I jumped for joy" to express their happiness? And
who has not understood what a person meant when they used
that phrase? It means they were happy.

On a practical level, the everyday use of either word to describe a positive emotion is acceptable. Communication is ef-

fected when both parties understand. And there is no misunderstanding when we use those words on a practical level. However, a closer examination of the use of these words in the Scriptures gives us a better understanding of their intended meaning, particularly for the Christian.

For the born-again believer, these words can never mean the same thing. We may still use both with impunity to express how we feel, but when it comes to expressing our faith and understanding of what we have in Christ Jesus, the two should never be confused.

Happiness is an emotion or an emotional state. It is reactive. When good things happen to us, we are happy. Conversely, when bad things happen, we are not happy. Consequently, we can say that happiness is fleeting. It comes and goes depending upon the circumstances in our lives. It is an emotional reaction to those circumstances.

Joy can be labeled an emotion, as well, but it is not reactive, at least not according to the Scriptures. Joy is lasting and immutable in the Christian's life, not fleeting, like happiness. In addition to being the second attribute of the fruit of the Spirit, we are told in **James 1:2**:

> *My brethren, count it all joy when ye fall*
> *into divers temptations.*

The Bible tells us that in our Christian experience, we are going to have various temptations. This does not mean that non-Christians do not have the same temptations. Of course they do. But Christians, by virtue of the Holy Spirit dwelling within them and effecting the transformation we spoke of above, are expected to avoid and resist temptations more than others.

A life of faith can be very tough during these times of testing. The Christian has not only their own conscience to deal with, but direct and unmistakable directions from the Bible and the ever-present convicting of the Holy Spirit within.

Sometimes, when the Lord is dealing with a believer's heart, or allowing adversity to facilitate our spiritual growth, the Christian experience can be quite unpleasant. I have never heard any of my fellow believers say, "I am so glad that God allowed this adversity to come into my life" as they underwent testing. That's because growing away from our flesh and toward spiritual things can be tough.

The truth is that times of testing are not happy times. We accept them without complaint, because we know that the Lord is working in our lives and only good can come from our challenges. Despite that assurance, the fact remains that we are not happy during times of testing. Happiness goes on hiatus, but here is the point: No matter how unhappy we may be, joy remains.

Is this verse in James telling us to be *happy* during our testing? No, it is not. In fact, by encouraging us to be *joyful* through the testing, the verse actually acknowledges that testing will make us unhappy. The real message is that while we are unhappy due to the circumstances in which we find ourselves, we can still have joy.

Happiness is dependent upon the circumstances of our lives. Joy is not. Joy is something we have irrespective of what happens in our lives, good or bad. Let me give you an example of what I mean.

In **Revelation 2:10**, we read these prophetic words written to the church at Smyrna regarding heavy persecution they were going to have to endure:

> *Fear none of those things which thou shalt suffer:*
> *behold, the devil shall cast some of you into*
> *prison, that you may be tried; and ye shall have*
> *tribulation ten days; be thou faithful unto death,*
> *and I will give thee a crown of life.*

This prophecy did not come true right away. But it *did* come true. In AD 156, some sixty years later, many of the deacons and leaders of the church at Smyrna were arrested and put into prison by the Roman oppressors. Their crime: supporting another King, a King who was no longer even alive on the earth, the Lord Jesus Christ.

In a period of ten days, just as God had prophesied, the leadership was jailed or killed, and the bishop of the church and aged apostolic father, the blessed Polycarpus, was brought before the Roman governor in the amphitheater where many had previously been slain for their faith.

Polycarpus was offered his freedom if he would but curse the name of this King Jesus. Without hesitation, he answered, "Eighty and six years I have served Him and He has done me nothing but good. How then shall I curse Him, my Lord and Savior?"

The bloodthirsty crowd cried for his death, and they began to lash him to the stake to be burned. Polycarpus begged them to let him stand unlashed so that he could show the power, grace, and joy of his Lord. His wishes were honored, and he stood and died without any attempt to escape.

Polycarpus certainly could not have been happy with his circumstances. The church he pastored was under attack, its leadership slaughtered, and now he was facing a most heinous death himself. But his unhappiness with the circumstances did not impact or impugn his spiritual joy. His joy was the fruit of the Spirit who indwelled him, and it was his strength in time of adversity.

Happiness is something we project when we feel good. Joy comes from knowing we are right with God because of our relationship with Jesus Christ. The former is fickle and fleeting; the latter is sure and lasting. We can be happy and joyful at the same time, but more importantly, when life's circumstances deal us a hard blow and we are unhappy, our joy is still intact.

What to Share with Your Child

Today was hard for all of us. Buddy was on all of our minds, but we had to do the things we had to do. You kids had school, and your mother and I had to go to work. But what helped me make it through my day was knowing that I would be with all of you this evening and that we would be able to be together and share the love we have for Buddy with each other.

I feel like we are honoring him when we spend time together remembering him. I hope you do, too, because I feel it is very important that we share the way we feel with each other and help each other.

I read something funny in the book I am reading to help us with these evening devotions, and I wanted to share it with you. I hope it makes you smile. It is okay to smile and feel good at the same time we feel hurt inside—that is really what our lesson is about tonight; and we will get to that in a moment. But first let me share this funny thought with you.

Sometimes, when we hear people speak in another language, the words they use sound a little funny to us, don't they? And sometimes, when they explain the meaning in English, the words sound a little backward or out of order.

Well, I think our English language must sound pretty funny to the other people, too. Sometimes the things we say must really confuse them. For instance, we call things that we transport in ships CARgo, but those same things transported on land are called a SHIPment.

The picture those words give to people just learning our language must seem very silly. And they probably wonder why we say that we park in the DRIVEway and drive on the PARKway. You know, when you think about it, it really does sound silly, doesn't it?

This evening we are going be talking about two other words that we sometimes confuse: happiness *and* joy. *What is happiness?*

Have your child(ren) give you their definition of *happiness*. If they have trouble coming up with a definition, help them along. You will find that it is almost impossible to define this word without using the word *joy*, but we want to avoid using that word, because our point is to show them the difference between the two words. The answer we are looking for would be something like, *"when I am glad and not sad."* Then give them some examples or illustrations to ensure that they understand.

That is a good definition, kids. Being happy is being glad. It is the opposite of being sad. If we like someone, we are happy when we see them. But if that person moves away and we don't see them much anymore, it makes us sad, right? If going to the amusement park makes us happy, but then the amusement park closes, that makes us sad.

So, our happiness depends on things that happen in our lives. Changes can make us sad. That is why we were happy when Buddy was with us, but now we are sad because that has changed and he has gone on ahead to heaven and lives there now. Our happiness changes when things change in our lives.

But joy is different. In the Bible verse that we are using for our devotions this week, **Galatians 5:22**, *the second thing it talks about is joy. Let's read that verse one more time. It says:*

But the fruit of the Spirit is love, joy, peace, long-suffering, gentleness, goodness, faith. . . .

Sometimes you hear people use the words joy *and* happiness *together, but they really do not mean the same thing. Remember, happiness is something that can change, but not joy. Let me explain. If we went on vacation to Disney World, that would make you very happy, wouldn't it?*

It would also bring you great joy to know we were going. But let's say that when we got there, it was pouring rain all day long and we were not able to go into the park. I think your happiness would turn to sadness very quickly, wouldn't it?

But the joy of going to the park would not be gone, because you knew that the next day you would still be able to go. On one hand, your happiness was gone, but on the other your joy would still be there. The same thing applies to Buddy. We are so unhappy that he got old and his life with us came to an end, but we have joy in knowing that he is well and young again and that we will see him again in heaven.

In chapter 16 of the book of John, Jesus was talking to His disciples about death, and He told them that death would make them weep, but that their sorrow would be turned into joy. That is the hope He gives us, for Buddy and for ourselves. We need to let our joy take over for happiness right now. We need to try to put aside the things that make us unhappy and remember why we have joy. It is something that God gives to us to help us when we have unhappy times. He wants us to know that He loves us and His animals, which was last night's lesson, and that should bring us great joy.

Chapter 17

DAY 3 DEVOTIONAL: PEACE

The third element of the fruit of the Holy Spirit is *peace.*

But the fruit of the Spirit is love, joy, peace, long-suffering, gentleness, goodness, faith. . . .

—*Galatians 5:22*

Peace is an extraordinary word. The accepted definition of the word, apart from a battlefield setting, is "freedom from disturbance; quiet and tranquility." The word is extraordinary, because it is used so frequently, often flippantly, but its fulfillment has been so utterly elusive. This world has never enjoyed the true peace. Since the Garden of Eden, there has never been a time of freedom from disturbance or absolute quiet and tranquility. In fact, even Eden was not at peace for long.

Perhaps no other concept has been as eagerly, yet so unsuccessfully sought after as peace. Love is attainable, and many have been successful in its pursuit. Joy is attainable. But peace remains the proverbial "carrot" for all mankind. We have had peace talks, peace conferences, peace treaties, peace offerings, and every other peace moniker effort you want to name, and nothing has resulted in lasting peace on this old planet.

Politicians promise peace as part of their campaign platforms, but they never deliver. For some it is just empty campaign rhetoric, but others actually endeavor to achieve this lofty goal with whatever factions seem to be against the nation at the time. Yet, in all of mankind's history, no one has yet succeeded. Peace is fleeting and thus far, unattainable.

But the Lord weighs in on this thing called peace. In **John 14:27**, we are told with certainty and authority:

> *Peace I leave with you, my peace I give unto you:*
> *not as the world giveth, give I unto you. Let not*
> *your heart be troubled, neither let it be afraid. . . .*

In one sweeping statement, God not only tells us that we can have His peace in our lives, but He acknowledges that the world's peace, the peace that man negotiates for and promises, is inferior to what He can give us. With the world's peace, there is always a cost. One side or both must give up something, make some sort of concession. With God, one need not do anything but accept the gift.

The peace that Jesus has promised is free from above. It is not something we must pray for and request. Jesus said He was going to leave it here for us when He left. Where is it, then? *What* is it? If we read the preceding text, we understand that

Jesus was going to send the Comforter, or Peacemaker, when He left. That Comforter is the Holy Spirit of God.

Believers are indwelt by God's Spirit. When we accept the Lord Jesus Christ as Savior, He takes up residence within us and becomes a permanent part of who we are. He is referred to as the divine, or new, nature that all Christians possess. And immediately the Holy Spirit begins His work within us, not complementing, but controlling our conscience and convicting us of the sinful things in our lives. He helps us to give up those hurtful things we have taken on, from bad habits to wrong attitudes.

But that is only half of His work. After He leads us to drop something bad from our lives, He simultaneously adds something good, nurturing the different aspects of fruit in our lives (i.e., love, joy, peace, etc.). And the peace that Jesus left with us manifests itself as personal peace with God. And when you are at peace with God, the whole world can be in turmoil, but your heart will still be calm.

It is this peace we need to tap in to for ourselves and for our children when we face sorrow in our lives. The world offers peace. You can join support groups or find therapists who specialize in pet loss, or whatever other issues you might face in life. But the peace they offer is usually temporal and incomplete.

Support groups can afford you friendly contacts with people who are experiencing, or who have experienced, the same pain you are feeling. There is a modicum of comfort in being able to share with someone who understands what you are going through. But after that person leaves the meeting, you are left with the same ache you had earlier. The same is true with a therapist. The same is true with me.

As an author who can understand your pain because I have been there so many times myself, I know what you are going through. I can offer a shoulder to cry on via my personal e-mail address on my website at www.coldnosesbook.com. I can give you tools and exercises to help you deal with your sorrow. But I have no magic button to push to rid you of your sorrow and to give you peace.

Readers can contact the author via his website at www.coldnosesbook.com.

I can only point you to the One whom I know who can and will help—the Lord. He and He alone can give you peace that a friend or therapist or I cannot give you. If you are a believer, that peace is already yours. All you have to do is tap in to it.

If you have not yet made a profession of faith in Jesus Christ, you can do that anytime you like. Just call on Him and ask Him to be your Lord and Savior. It is not difficult. There is no secret handshake, no magic decoder ring. It is just realizing your need for God and asking Him into your heart.

The peace of God is unfathomable, and consequently, nearly impossible to explain more or better than I have here. The Bible itself tells us in **Philippians 4:7**:

And the peace of God, which passeth all understanding, shall keep your hearts and minds through Christ Jesus.

Where peace is found in the world, you will also find that the things that impede and undermine it are also present, namely, suspicion and apprehension. Both parties to a peace agreement—be they individuals, groups, or nations—are happy to make peace with their enemies, but they do so with great concern as to the honesty and integrity of the ones with whom they are entering into that agreement. Perceived ulterior motives and intent are usually considerations that delay or even nix agreements.

Nations draft long, detailed, and specific treaties with built-in safeguards to prevent other nations from violating their trust. Invariably, these agreements are ratified by official representatives of several other "watchdog" or "witness" nations to ensure the details are binding.

In divorce settlements, a legal agreement is first negotiated and then signed by both parties to ensure that one or the other does not renege or change their mind. Of course, there are potentially many other factors at work in a divorce that are not present with a peace treaty, but the goals for both are the same. In any agreement, each party wants to safeguard its own interests and welfare while fostering the peace.

Basically, the peace that the world offers is reconciliatory. Nations seek peace to end differences or wars. People seek peace to end conflict and ill feelings. All parties make concessions and allowance to accommodate the interests of the other parties, offer at least a halfhearted apology for past behavior and transgressions, and try to make nice from then on with each other.

God's peace is not like that. In fact, to quote a portion of the verse above, He says of the peace He offers, "Not as the world giveth, give I unto you . . ." (John 24:27). In our reconciliation with God, we meet His demands . . . period. There is no negotiation. There is no concession on God's part. We must believe, repent, and receive forgiveness His way. There are no preconditions for God to meet. The agreement is one-sided; we agree to God's terms and yield to His will.

Now, anyone with any business or political sense will tell you that this is not the way to negotiate. It is a fool's errand, because you give your opponent all the advantage and clout. But God is not an opponent. God is on our side. He is for us. His terms give an advantage to us.

In His benevolence, after we agree to His terms, He welcomes us to His family as adopted children. He bestows upon us all the inheritance that He gives to His only begotten Son. He regenerates us and places His Holy Spirit within us. The Spirit then works to manifest the fruits of love, joy, peace, long-suffering, etc., in us. Peace is a benefit to our reconciliation with God, not a fulfillment of a condition or term.

God's peace is very personal. He takes the fears and apprehensions of our hearts and erases them. He sets the crooked straight in our minds and relieves the anxieties and stresses that commonly plague the human heart and mind.

I recall my life before I met the Lord Jesus. It was a time toward the end of America's infamous Cold War with the Soviet Union. I remember well the issues that caused me constant stress and worry:

- Will there be nuclear war?
- Will my children survive to live out their lives?

- Will I get cancer?
- Will America last?

When I finally came to the point in my life where I understood what Jesus did for me and how very much I needed Him in my life, I bowed my head and received Him. It didn't take me long. It wasn't really very eventful. I didn't hear angels singing, and the earth did not move beneath my feet (actually I was on my knees, but I think you get the point). But when I raised my head and opened my eyes, I knew something was different.

Immediately, I knew God was real. I had only suspected it before and I had leaned in that direction, but this one act of faith in asking Him into my life cleared the conduit from God to my heart and opened my spiritual eyes. And I knew! And not only that, but that *"know so"* feeling erased my fears.

They were gone. Just that quickly, they no longer worried me, because I knew God was real and alive. And somehow that made me also know that He was in control and I had nothing in life to fear. I had instant and lasting peace. Over forty years later, that peace has never changed or wavered.

How anyone can go through life without this peace that God gives is beyond me. I understand that some are in the dark and are not aware that it exists, but shouldn't they be looking for it, as you and I had? If they were, God would make sure they found it, too.

I hope you can join me in thanking God that we can have His peace and that it is not a fickle or fleeting peace of the world's variety. It is important that we portray God's peace properly and emphatically to our children, and we can only do that if we epit-omize it for them.

It is not enough for us to tell them that we feel God's peace; they need to see it in our lives. They need to see that our joy perseveres even when we are unhappy and that the peace of God reigns over our fears, anxieties, and stress.

What to Share with Your Child

Begin this evening's devotion by asking your children a few questions. They need to take an active part in this meeting of the family. Don't pressure them or scold them if things don't go ex-actly the way you planned for them to go. Just lighten up and allow the time together to unfold in whatever way it does. Guide the conversation when you can, but allow them to speak and con-tribute, too. They might even ask a few questions of their own, so be prepared, and in every social setting, if you don't know the an-swers, tell them that you don't and that you will get back to them.

Let's start tonight's time together with a couple of questions, okay?

What does the word peace *mean, and can you give me an ex-ample of when peace happens?*

Let your child(ren) answer before you continue. Acknowledge their definition and correct it if it is not quite right. Then move on to their example(s) of when peace happens. The most com-mon answer will be, "Peace happens after war or after an argu-ment." Confirm that this is correct and then move on with the following:

Yes, peace does come after war. That is a very good answer. I wish that there weren't wars, but it is good that we get peace from war. And yes, peace does come after an argument. Sometimes when you argue with your friends (or your sisters and brothers), you get a little upset and angry, but eventually you work things out and there is peace again, right?

Those are good examples of when peace comes. But peace can also just be a quiet time. You have heard the term peace and quiet. That just means that there isn't a lot of noise, like music or traffic or dogs barking, and you can just sit and think in peace.

It is kind of like when you are in a canoe on a lake and it is so quiet. The wind is not blowing and you are far away from cars and people. You are just lying back in the boat as it floats on the lake and you are looking at the clouds above. It is very peaceful and very nice. That is a different type of peace from the peace that comes after a war.

When you are in a canoe and it is so quiet . . .

Do you remember that Christmas song that you like so much . . . "Silent Night"? That song talks about this kind of peace. The words start out:

(You might sing it softly to them.)

Silent night, holy night,
All is calm, all is bright . . .

And then how does the chorus go? Sing with me . . .

Sleep in heavenly peace,
Sleep in heavenly peace.

Heaven is a place of perfect peace. There is:

- 🐾 *No fear*
- 🐾 *No crime*
- 🐾 *No anger*
- 🐾 *No yelling*
- 🐾 *And nothing to upset us*

Isn't it wonderful to know that our Buddy is there right now, enjoying all of that? And one day we will be there, too. It will be very peaceful to be there with Buddy and to share the love that we have for him and that he has for us.

*But we don't have to wait. We can have peace like that right now. In **John 14:27** God tells us about that peace. He said it was not like the peace the world gives, but it was a heavenly peace that* *only those who trust Him can have. We know we have that peace of God's when we think about Buddy and feel good to know he is happy and at rest. That is God telling our hearts not to fear.*

I think this is a good time for us to remember something about Buddy and share it with the rest of the family. And don't forget to tell us something you think is in heaven that has made Buddy happy.

Chapter 18

DAY 4 DEVOTIONAL: LONG-SUFFERING

The fourth element of the fruit of the Holy Spirit is *long-suffering*.

> *But the fruit of the Spirit is love, joy, peace, long-suffering, gentleness, goodness, faith. . . .*
>
> —*Galatians 5:22*

This word *long-suffering* is one of several words we find in the Bible that appear to mean one thing, but actually mean something completely different. Our first thought about this word could be that it means to suffer for a long time. It does not. The word is actually made up of two Greek words that mean "long" and "temper." By combining these, we get the word *long-tempered*.

The word *suffer* in the King James Version of the Bible can also mean "to allow." Together, these very similar definitions can speak to self-restraint and patience. So the actual meaning of our key word this evening could properly be translated to mean "to allow for a long time."

For clarification, I should tell you that I use the King James Version of the Bible. I use this version or translation by choice. The study of the inspiration and preservation of the Scriptures was one of my pet projects in college, and as a result of my studies, I opted to use this translation above all others. In my opinion, it is the most faithful and trustworthy of all translations. I will not take the time to explain why here, as that would take us far off topic, but I would be happy to explain my position if you wish to contact me at the e-mail address provided earlier in the book.

I understand that many people do not like the old English vernacular that is used in this translation. Some refer to the language used as "Elizabethan" or "Victorian" English, even "Shakespearian." But it would seem to predate even those styles. Even Shakespeare used a more modern version of English. Personally, I have come to enjoy the *thees* and *thous* and I feel very comfortable when I read it. For me, how we came by this translation is much more important than the style of English used.

That notwithstanding, I cannot deny that some of the meanings of the words add a little more adventure and challenge for the reader. For instance, the word *conversation* almost always translates to "behavior" and the word *let* often means "hinder," which is just about the direct opposite of what the face value of the word appears to be.

There can be tricky moments when reading the King James Version to be sure, but usually our modern understanding of the meaning of these words gives us pause as we read the ancient application. That is our signal that perhaps the word has a different modern meaning. A quick glance at the comments in the margins of the Bible we are using usually sheds light on any unusual word's meaning and clears up any confusion.

Variations of the application of the meaning of this word *longsuffering* are acceptable. Often it means "to allow for a long time," but it can also mean "having patience" or "being slow to anger." All of these applications have similar intent, and they can be used interchangeably without any real damage to the meaning.

If you would permit me, for the purpose of this devotional, I am going to use the "slow to anger" application. I think this definition fits our needs a little better than the others. We will not ignore the other definitions, but I want to primarily focus on the anger aspect.

There are a lot of angry people in this world who act out their anger and frustrations in very heinous and hurtful ways, such as:

- 🐾 Terrorism
- 🐾 School shootings
- 🐾 Movie theater assaults
- 🐾 Road rage
- 🐾 A host of other senseless acts

Granted, some of these perpetrators are mentally unstable or are acting upon a hateful religious ideology, but many are not. They are just angry. For whatever reasons or circumstances, many feel cheated by life or other people and, in their self-centered bubble of anger and frustration, they seek what they consider to be justice by striking out in a shocking, attention-getting way.

Unfortunately, they usually wind up meting out injustice to innocent people.

These types of people are certainly not slow to anger. In fact, anger appears to be their immediate option of choice. Laws, justice, and social bearing do not seem to be qualities that rate very high in their warped outlook on life.

Left unchecked, this is the effect that anger can have on anyone. Anger brings out the evil that is our human nature at its worst. Reason and logic are ignored as this powerful emotion rises up within us and takes control. And if we lose control, as we have seen over and over again, terrible things happen.

That being said, there is nary a one among us who does not experience anger in our lives. Each of us faces pain, grief, unfairness, and injustice at one time or another. Few of us are able to completely subdue the feelings of anger that we experience when we are wronged.

For example, you are a great driver. You have never gotten a ticket, because you never speed and you always obey the rules of the road. One day an impatient young man behind you expresses his anger at you going only the speed limit, and as he passes you in the left lane, which just opened up, he draws your attention to one of his uplifted fingers and tries to scare you by pretending he is going to run his car into yours.

Even though it was just a bluff, you, of course, react by quickly moving your vehicle to the shoulder of the road. A policeman, who just pulled up behind you in traffic, and who did not see the threat made to you just moments earlier, pulls you over and tickets you for hazardous or dangerous driving. Really?

Things like this happen all the time in life. On the football field, it is usually the guy who reacts to being punched or pushed down who draws the penalty, not the guy who started it. It is unfair, but it is almost expected. And often, no amount of explaining will change the result. It can be so frustrating.

Your family lost a precious pet. No amount of anger will bring him or her back. We can play the circumstances over and over again in our minds, review and second-guess all that the veterinarian did or said, and repeatedly ask God, "Why?" but nothing is going to change the situation. It can seem so unfair sometimes, and we get so angry and so frustrated.

I suppose this is a normal reaction to unfairness. Disappointment is another reaction we may have. It is a form of anger, but with a bit of temperance added to it. Some of us even get angry at or disappointed in God. Perhaps you feel that way right now— a little put out that God would allow this trauma and grief to befall your family. It might help you to know that this author is no stranger to such feelings.

Years ago I had a precious Chihuahua named Pebbles. She was a wonder and a blessing in my life. But I suppose each of us can say the same thing about our dogs, cats, and other pets. And like most pets, Pebbles had one endearing antic she pulled that always got my attention. I would be sitting on the sofa or in a chair, and she would slide under my feet on her back, work her way literally under my foot, and push up and balance my foot with her four paws. It was so cute and memorable.

Because of a medical condition, we were not able to get Pebbles spayed right away. Tests showed that she would have a negative reaction to the anesthesia. It took many years of a doctor's care and testing before he finally said she was ready for the simple procedure. I was happy to hear she could finally get this work done, as her being in heat really took a toll on her—and on our carpets.

Although the veterinarian assured me that she should be fine, I made it a matter of prayer for a few weeks before agreeing to the surgery. As a result of my earnest prayers, I was comforted in my heart about the procedure. I cannot tell you how I knew God was telling me to proceed; I just knew. It was just that still, small voice that God uses to speak to His children—and within, I felt peace that all would be well.

So we proceeded. I made the appointment. She would need the whole day at the veterinarian's office to recover, so I dropped her off, imploring the doctor to keep in constant contact with me until she was fine, and then I went to work. I had full trust that all was going to be well, just as I had been impressed to feel.

Imagine my shock just an hour later, when the veterinarian called and, speaking in a distressed, high-pitched voice, informed me that Pebbles had passed away unexpectedly. It was devastating—not just because of my grief, but because of my disappointment in God. I felt I had been betrayed.

But I was not angry. I was a seasoned enough Christian to know that Romans 8:28 still applied, that God would bring good from all of this. I didn't know how that could possibly happen, but I knew it would. Somehow God would use this traumatic experience to glorify Himself and bring about something good.

Time passed, and my pain healed a bit. My expectation that God would bring something good from the pain also passed. But years later, after I had authored *Cold Noses at the Pearly Gates*, a reader wrote and said:

Dear Gary:

I know you do not know me, but I felt led from God to write to you and tell you that if it had not been for your Pebbles passing unexpectedly, I am certain you would have never written this wonderful book and I would never have come to know the Lord as my own. The Lord used your Pebbles to save my soul.

Wow, I was stunned! I was both happy and ashamed at the same time: happy to know that the Lord did not betray me, and ashamed to have thought that He had. This woman would be the first of many to make the same observation over the years that followed. They and the Lord were such a blessing and encouragement to me.

I have never forgotten how quick I was to blame God for the bad that came into my life. And I have been able to see the same snap judgment in others who contact me to question why God would allow such things to happen nor do such things to them. I, and they, need to remember that God never visits bad things upon us. He wishes only good upon us. And when the world, or Satan, or even we ourselves bring chaos or calamity into our lives, God promises that He will bring good from it, just as He did with the passing of my Pebbles.

Hopefully it will help you—and through you, your children—to know that your pain is not unique. You are not alone. Life did not single you out. We all suffer from the same evils and woes in this world. I used to feel alone in my pain, until thousands of readers wrote to me and I realized that I was not alone. Knowing that we are not alone in our suffering and pain can be an un-expected balm to our hearts, so I wanted you to know this.

And hopefully you will pass that thought on to your children. Children respond more readily to group dynamics than adults. That is why salespeople can so easily cash in on fads and trends among youth. Knowing that everyone feels the same pain over the loss of their respective pets will give them a sense of nor-malcy in a time that is far from normal.

Please impress your children with the understanding that God is not to blame for the passing of their cherished pet, but that He will use it to touch their lives in some way—a good way. It may not happen right away, but, as in my case, it will happen. They need to keep their faith that God loves them and is look-ing out for them. We will take a more detailed look at that word *faith* in our Day 7 devotion, but suffice it to say here that God is pleased when we look to Him during times of hardship and grief and when we trust in Him.

What to Share with Your Child

This is day four of our meeting together as a family to have de-votions. I may not have explained to you before exactly what a de-votion is, so I will do it now.

A devotion, or a devotional time, is just a very short and spe-cial time when we meet together as a family to share our love and support for each other. We look into the Bible for guidance and encouragement from God and we talk about the things He says.

We are showing our love for God by showing that we love each other enough to spend time together learning something new from His Word. We are "devoting" our time to Him and seeking His help. I have enjoyed these nightly meetings with our family. So far we have talked about love, joy, and peace, and tonight we will be looking at a word that is a little harder to understand: long-suffering.

It has been nice spending time with all of you during these evenings. Sometimes we get so busy with other things and friends that it is hard to find the time for family. So this has been wonderful, wouldn't you agree?

The devotions we are sharing will only last seven days, but I was hoping that you have enjoyed them as much as I have and that we might continue to have our own devotions after we are finished with these. Would you like that, kids?

- ❧ If the children react positively, fantastic! There are devotionals available online or in your local Christian bookstores. Undoubtedly, if you asked your pastor, he could probably give you some materials to follow, as well.

- ❧ If the children hesitate in their response to you, or if they seem reluctant, quickly offer a compromise (i.e., "Well, maybe we could just start by having them once or twice a week? After all, they don't last that long and being together is so nice, isn't it?").

Now, let's get to tonight's word. It is the word long-suffering. *You would think by the sound of it that it means to suffer for a long time—like we all did that day when that skunk sprayed Buddy. Do you remember that? We all had to pitch in washing him and giving him a haircut. Yuck, what a day that was! Boy, did we all suffer.*

NOTE: Obviously, as I warned you earlier, this is story to use as an example. I am confident that you will be able to replace it with a story your own family can shares of a time when you felt you suffered together.

But to suffer long is not what this word means. The real meaning is going to surprise you. It means to have "patience" or to be "slow to anger." I usually share a Bible verse with you during each devotion, but tonight I am just going to tell you what the Bible says, because the words are hard to understand.

What the Bible teaches in both the Old and New Testaments is that God is long-suffering toward us. He looks down on us and sees the bad things that we do and they make Him sad. But because He loves us, He is patient and slow to get angry with us.

It is kind of like when I keep after you to clean your room—

[or you could use another example that applies and to which your children can relate]

—but you forget or you just don't want to do it right away. I could get angry and punish you, but because I love you, I am very patient and very slow to get angry with you.

So, God sets a perfect example for us. When we see how patient He is with us and how slow He is to get angry at the things we do, maybe we should treat Him the same way that He treats us. Maybe we should not get angry at Him as quickly as we sometimes do.

When we lost Buddy, we were very sad. We knew he was old

and that he had lived a wonderful long life. But even though he was ready to go on ahead, we weren't really ready to let him go, were we? But there was nothing we could do. So, we turned to God and said, "Why, God? Why did You let this happen to Buddy?"

We kind of blamed God, didn't we? Do you think that was fair to God? After all, He brought Buddy to us and Buddy had a great life with us. But his age caught up with him, as it does with all living things, and his body got old. It was just natural.

Don't you think we owe God the same patience as He shows us? Don't you think that we should be slow to get angry at God? How can we be angry that Buddy gets to see heaven already? As I said, God gave Buddy a wonderful life with us. Now He has given him an even better life. I think we should close the lesson tonight by being long-suffering toward God and thanking Him for giving Buddy a new life.

Okay, let's change it up tonight. Instead of a thought about Buddy, let's each share with the family the first thing you are going to say to Buddy when you see him one day later on. As for me, I am going to tell him, "Buddy, you didn't know this, but you helped the family get closer and stronger. When you left us, we realized how much we loved you, and the sadness of losing you made us come together and help each other. Thank you, Buddy." How about somebody else—what are you going to say to Buddy?

I think this is a good time for us to remember something about Buddy and share it with the rest of the family. Let's end tonight's devotion by naming something you think is making Buddy happy right now.

Chapter 19

DAY 5 DEVOTIONAL: GENTLENESS

The fifth element of the fruit of the Holy Spirit is *gentleness*.

But the fruit of the Spirit is love, joy, peace, long-suffering, gentleness, goodness, faith. . . .

—Galatians 5:22

If you were to look up the definition of *gentle*, you would find that the dictionary gives this response: "a quiet and meek spirit or attitude." Jesus was meek, and He said it was the preferred attitude for anyone wishing to represent Him. He said that we ought to make it our goal to develop a meek spirit and attitude. The world is in direct contrast with His view. The world thinks meekness, or gentleness, is weakness. That is so far from the truth.

Again, Jesus was meek, but He was far from being weak, or the kind of person at whom bullies kick sand. I want to share with you an accurate account of what Jesus endured, something quite different from the watered-down, cute picture many paint regarding the torture and death of Jesus Christ.

I certainly do not recommend, nor do I want you to share this with your children, but I want to share it with you in the hopes that the stark reality of what the Lord endured for us will exponentially increase your desire to teach this trait of meekness, or gentleness, to your children.

Weak, indeed! Just look at the physical endurance He had to muster to become our atonement for sin. He was repeatedly beaten and roughed up by the Roman soldiers, men who were notoriously tough and cruel. They spat at Him, smote Him, and tore the beard from His face. They placed a crown of thorns on His head and pressed it down so that the two-inch-plus thorns buried into His skull. All the while He reviled them not, but He endured.

They whipped Him with the Roman equivalent to a cat-o'-nine tails. At the end of each strand of the whip, they tied pieces of metal or bones, the objective being to tear human flesh and inflict grave bodily damage. The Bible says in Isaiah of Jesus that His visage, or appearance, was so marred that He didn't even look like a man. He was ripped and bloodied so badly that His flesh was hanging off Him.

After all this physical torment, coupled with His not receiving either sustenance or water, they placed a massive, heavy cross on His back and made Him carry or drag it to what would be His place of death. He endured this for quite a while before assistance was required, His waning strength was evidence that He had allowed Himself to suffer in His human flesh rather than rely on His power as the Son of God.

After all of this, they laid Him out on that cross and hammered His hands and feet to it with enormous, painful spikes. Once He was fastened securely, they raised that large, heavy cross up and dropped it into the hole provided for it with a thud. The Bible tells us that every bone and joint of His body was dislodged due to that painful and evil process. And still He held up and was able to offer forgiveness and compassion to others.

I am an undefeated third-degree black belt in Shodokan karate, and I used to tag alligators and catch diamondback rattlers for the state of Florida. I lift weights and jog. I suppose all of this makes me "manly" in the world's eyes. But I submit to you, I could not have held up as Jesus did. Few, if any, could. How anyone could consider His meek spirit an indication that He was weak is outrageous. They are either dishonest or delusional.

A meek heart means that we are gentle toward others, not cowardly or afraid. It means that we are strong enough to endure injustice or assault without striking back in anger or vengeance. It doesn't mean we are doormats, either. We can certainly stand up for our rights and interests; we can protect ourselves, our loved ones, and our property; but we do so in order. We try to get along with others in every way, as Jesus did, before we ultimately have to take harsher action.

Our purpose here, however, is to teach children about gentleness. It would seem that this would be one of the toughest of the seven traits, or elements, we are addressing this week to teach them. But, in my mind, based on my experience, it should be the easiest of the seven. Children are the champions of gentleness. They have such trusting and tender hearts. Who among us has not heard the scream or cry of a child when we have stepped on a beetle or a spider: "No, don't kill him! What if he has children?" or words to that effect?

That children naturally possess this meek and tender spirit is evidenced even by nature. When a five-year-old boy fell into a gorilla enclosure in New Jersey in 1986 and was knocked unconscious, a male gorilla by the name of Jambo, a dozen times stronger than the manliest man, rushed to the aid of the child, gently sweeping him up into its arms, protecting him from the more playful and reckless young gorillas in the pen until help arrived.

Had it been a teenager or an adult who fell in, the result might have been more tragic. But even this potentially ferocious male gorilla perceived the tenderness of the child. And this was no fluke, for a few years later it happened again with a three-year-old who fell into an enclosure where Binti, a female gorilla, duplicated Jambo's efforts.

To everyone's amazement, the gorilla was gentle. . . .

I have heard all sorts of explanations as to why these gorillas treated these children so gently. Some suppose it was paternal or maternal instinct. Maybe, but there is no evidence to suggest that. The same gorilla displayed little tolerance for the young of its own species.

Others suppose it was just the children's good fortune that they fell in on days when the gorillas were in good moods. I suppose that is possible, but there is no record of them having "bad days" when their moods were less than stellar.

Still others say that these two gorillas were accustomed to humans and enjoyed human presence, to the point of great tolerance. Again, maybe, but I think it is a lot simpler than that. I think gentleness begets gentleness. Animals, especially primates, are extremely perceptive. While we watch them at the zoos and parks, they are watching us, too. They see how we treat our young. They see that we are gentle and protective. They also see that our children are tender and gentle. Children pose no threat to them, short of tossing a peanut or two at them once in a while.

This gentleness, coupled with their innocence and tender hearts, is why the Lord used children as the example of what kind of people heaven would be populated by: people with child-like faith and gentleness. This is one of the elements of the fruit of the Holy Spirit, something God wants to develop within us so that we have that childlike faith and gentle spirit.

During this time of bereavement, we need to put ourselves in the place of our child. As we observed earlier, adults can be traumatized by the loss of the family pet just as easily and just as severely as a child. But adults, by virtue of their age, have acquired experience over the years that helps them cope with grief and sorrow. Repeated exposure to these emotions make them far better equipped to cope emotionally and mentally.

But the heart that weeps for the demise of a pesky, even potentially dangerous, insect hardly has the wherewithal to put the loss of their best friend in adult perspective. Indeed, the loss of someone they have played with, clung to, and allowed to sleep on their bed can be, and often is, a crushing emotional blow.

Long-suffering and patience from yesterday's lesson are good tools for parents to use when helping their gentle-hearted child accept the passing of their best friend, or any animal or even humans for that matter. Children are going to feel a sad event deeper and more severely than you or I. They need understanding and patience in these matters. We cannot be flippant on this point; we must understand this and be proactive in these areas.

I am haunted to this day by a traumatic night in my life from when I was a very young child. I believe I was eight or nine years old. My family was driving through Georgia one evening, on our way to my father's new duty station in Florida. I am not sure where we were in Georgia.

What I do recall is that there were an extraordinary number of rabbits on the highway that night. I am not exaggerating when I say we saw several hundred in our headlights in a period of about twenty minutes, the time it took before I convinced my mother to demand my dad stop for the evening.

I became aware of the rabbits when my dad hit the first one. I jumped up and looked out the windshield from the backseat. He cursed and said "blankety-blank rabbit." And then another one darted in front of the car. I was mortified: Every thirty seconds or so, another rabbit would run out into the road in front of us. Most made it across, but unfortunately, several did not.

It was horrifying to me. I screamed when my dad hit each one, and I cried uncontrollably when he would not stop or slow down. The event was extremely emotional for me, but it was made so much worse by my father's callous disregard for the rabbits and my trauma. As I said earlier, my mother eventually saw the impact all of this was having on me and finally took control of the situation.

My father is gone now, and I miss him. I loved him, of course, but we never really had a close relationship, and I believe it was because of what happened that one night. As I said, I loved my dad, but I did not respect him. I saw a cruelty in him that I did not like. We did not share the same love for animals, and that was okay. But he held no respect for them, either, and that callous spirit came across to me as a youngster and put a wall between us.

As parents, we need to recognize and constantly be aware of the tenderness of a child's heart. Oh, I am not saying that children cannot be cruel. Of course they can, and often to each other. But when it comes to pets, or animals in general, most kids have a very soft spot for them, and we parents need to cater to that part of them when circumstances dictate. The words to an Otis Redding song come to mind; "Try a little tenderness. . . ." Good advice.

What to Share with Your Child

*Kids, I want to share with you our key verse again. It is **Galatians 5:22** and it says . . . "But the fruit of the Spirit is love, joy, peace, longsuffering, gentleness, goodness, faith. . . ."*

We are going to talk about the word gentleness *this evening. Who can tell me what that word means?*

Give the child(ren) time to think and respond, and be positive about any answer they give you, finding a way to blend their definition into the right one. For example, if your child says, "Well, gentleness is when you are kind," that is not really what the word means, but you can respond like this, for instance:

Well, that is a very good guess. Gentle people are very kind people. And Jesus said that we should all be kind to one another and gentle. So those two words go together.

Who can give me an example of what gentleness is?

They will probably say something like "petting a cat" or "feeding a stray cat." Once again, be very positive and acknowledge their contribution and ideas.

That was an excellent example. May I share a story about gentleness with you, too? This is a very good story, one that you will like. It happened a long time ago, before you were born, but people still talk about it today because it was so amazing.

A young boy, just about your age(s), was at the zoo with his parents, and he leaned over the railing of the gorilla exhibit too far. You remember how I always tell you not to lean over rails, right? Well, I am sure his mommy told him the same thing, but he just didn't listen this day, and guess what happened?

Yes, that is right—he fell right over the railing and into the gorilla enclosure, which was down real low so the gorillas could not get out. He fell so far that he was actually knocked out when he hit the ground. And it gets worse.

As soon as he hit the ground with a thud, the big male gorilla heard the noise and came quickly over to where the boy had fallen. Everyone thought the little boy was in great danger, so they started yelling for the gorilla to leave him alone. They were shouting the gorilla's name: "Jambo, no, no. Leave the boy alone. Stay away from him."

But Jambo didn't listen. Instead, he went right over to the boy, and seeing that he was hurt, he gently picked the boy up and cuddled him in his arms until the zookeepers could come in and help.

That was an amazing act of gentleness, wasn't it? In **Mark 10–14**, we have a story about Jesus and some children. Their parents had brought the children to Jesus to be blessed by the Lord, but His disciples tried to keep them from seeing the Lord. I don't know why. They weren't being mean: they probably just didn't want too many people crowding Jesus. But Jesus told them not to stop the children from coming to Him. Here is what He said to the disciples:

> But when Jesus saw it, he was much displeased,
> and said unto them, Suffer the little children to
> come unto me, and forbid them not: for of such is
> the kingdom of God.

What Jesus was saying was that He wanted the disciples to allow the children to come to Him, because the people who loved Jesus were like those children. He meant that people had to be gentle and kindhearted. And that is why our word for this evening is gentleness. God wants us to be gentle people.

We cannot let things that hurt us, like the death of our beloved Buddy, take away our gentleness. If we get angry at God, or if we just get angry at this world and life on earth for being so painful at times, our gentleness will start to disappear. And we may become grumpy, like one of the seven dwarfs in Snow White. We don't want that to happen, and neither does God. That is why He has His Spirit inside us, teaching us how to be gentle and how to stay that way.

When we face hardships in our lives, we need to remember this. And we do face a lot of scary and painful things sometimes don't we? Like:

- 🐾 Losing a pet like Buddy
- 🐾 Bullies at school
- 🐾 Bees and wasps
- 🐾 Homework and tests

Instead of trying to remember something about Buddy and sharing that with each other tonight, let's each think of one thing that Buddy might say to us when we get to heaven. I will go first, if that is okay.

I think Buddy is going to want to talk about all that he has seen and done up there. He will probably describe all of these things and want to show them to us. What do you think?

Chapter 20

Day 6 Devotional: Goodness

The sixth element of the fruit of the Holy Spirit is *goodness*.

But the fruit of the Spirit is love, joy, peace, long-suffering, gentleness, goodness, faith. . . .

—Galatians 5:22

Of all the elements of the fruit of the Spirit that we are discussing this week, goodness would seem to be the most straightforward and the easiest to address. It would seem that everyone understands the difference between good and bad. We may all draw the dividing line between the two in different places, but the point is, there is a dividing line for everyone. Even those who choose to purposely do bad, consciously know they are crossing the line between right and wrong.

People know the difference between good and bad. As we discussed in chapter 2, each of us has a built-in conscience. The definition that Webster gives us is "an inner feeling or voice viewed as acting as a guide to the rightness or wrongness of one's behavior." Regardless of how numb our sense of right or wrong may become due to purposeful bad behavior, each of us is equipped with this factory-issued moral apparatus.

Unfortunately, that moral compass does not actually engage or turn on right away inside people. Young children lack the ability to discern the difference between good and bad. They learn quickly, but there are several years that parents must endure before their child's conscience is fully functional. Progress varies dependent upon many external factors.

All young children are born with that old, sinful, self-centered nature, which I think we all will admit is predominant until they learn the difference between right and wrong and the ramifications for each. You may not agree with me on this, but the evidence is plain for all to see.

Young children are bent on having their own way. They act in ways that older children and adults would never act, like throwing tantrums and making public spectacles of themselves for something as simple as not being able to be the one to push the shopping cart.

How many of you mothers or fathers had to climb into your child's crib and teach them how to scream and cry and carry on? None, I am sure. They already know how to do that on their own. They come out of the womb bawling and squalling, bent on getting their own way.

They don't care if you get enough sleep because of their crying all night. They don't care if you get angry. They don't care if they embarrass you in public. They only know what they want.

It is human nature without a fully developed conscience. It is typical toddler behavior. They want their own way, every time all the time, and they are not interested in negotiation.

Many years ago, I was at the store with my mother and younger brother. My younger brother wanted a toy fire engine. My mother told him he could not have it. He waited until we got to the cash register and then let out an unearthly wail, screaming, "My mommy hit me really hard because I wanted a toy. She hit me and hit me."

This was, of course, very unexpected and very embarrassing to my mother, as there were a lot of people we knew present. It didn't help that my brother had some bruises on him from having fallen a few days earlier. So, what do you think happened?

No, Mom did not buy him that toy. Instead, she pacified him by promising him that he could play with my toy fire engine at home, one of a collection I had acquired over several years and kept in immaculate condition. Now *I* felt like throwing a tantrum, but of course, I was too old for that. My conscience was in full working order, and I would not do that to my mother.

My point to all of this is to say that while this word *goodness* may seem like a very easy concept to discuss with your family, if you have younger children it may not resonate as clearly with them as with older children. There is that *"age of accountability"* factor with younger children, and it is a considerably problematic factor.

On the off chance that you are not familiar with this term, it is simply a belief, based upon solid, unimpeachable principles in the Bible that young children are unable to discern the difference between right and wrong until they reach a certain age. Until they reach this age, they are not accountable for their personal sins. That age has come to be called by Christians the *"age of accountability."*

It is widely accepted that children who have not reached this age are "innocents" who cannot discern the differences between right and wrong as readily as adults. Consequently, God does not hold them accountable as He does adults and older children. This godly principle and understanding of youthful innocence is even reflected in the laws of our land. Until a child reaches adulthood, they are not held accountable as adults are, and they usually receive a lesser sentence or punishment.

In terms of spiritual accountability, young children are considered "safe" in the Lord until they reach that age when they are accountable for their own actions and behaviors. Some set a certain age on this condition, such as nine or twelve. But the majority opinion is that the age varies with each child, depending upon their individual growth to maturity, which itself is dependent upon many outside factors and influences.

It is also widely accepted that there is also an allowance for adults who suffer any number of mental and/or intellectual impediments, who, for all practical purposes, have only the perceptions and understandings of younger children. They, too, are considered innocents and are safe under the grace of God and not accountable for their personal sins.

Though there is no specific verse that addresses this age of accountability issue, it is a logical and reasonable position to take when one considers the love and benevolence of God. The belief is based upon principles, but this does not diminish its credibility. That God would hold innocent children responsible is just preposterous, bordering on heartless legalism. It simply is not in keeping with God's revelation of Himself as the God of love, nor is it reflected in His Word. In fact, just the opposite is true.

We learned the meaning of the word *long-suffering* on day four of this devotional series. God epitomizes the definition of the word. In **2 Peter 3:9**, that long-suffering love is expressed in God's patience for our frail ways. We are told, "The Lord is not slack concerning his promise, as some men count slackness, but is longsuffering toward us, not willing that any should perish, but that all should come to repentance." God's will, God's very desire, is that no one would perish, speaking, of course, of the second, or eternal, death.

Now then, if we were to believe that God would not make provision for those who were too young emotionally and intellectually to see their need for repentance, could this teaching of

His long-suffering and unwillingness for any to perish be true? Anyone with any modicum of spiritual discernment would have to honestly admit that it could not. So, we are left with accepting the verse at face value: that God is, indeed, unwilling for anyone to perish.

If that was all the evidence we had, it would be difficult to embrace this belief about the age of accountability. But we have much more. Here are just a few passages from the New Testament that give credence to the position that children are innocent in the eyes of the Lord. From these verses, we see that Jesus, in His wonderful, unfathomable grace, obviously does not hold young children accountable.

But Jesus said, Suffer little children, and forbid them not, to come unto me: for of such is the kingdom of heaven.

—Matthew 19:14

And said, Verily I say unto you, Except ye be converted, and become as little children, ye shall not enter into the kingdom of heaven.

—Matthew 18:3

For the unbelieving husband is sanctified by the wife, and the unbelieving wife is sanctified by the husband: else were your children unclean; but now are they holy.

—1 Corinthians 7:14

Clearly, Jesus used the children who happened to be in His presence at the moment as a teaching aid, a visual example of innocence. His words cannot be misconstrued; He stated emphatically that the residents of heaven are to be exactly as those children (and, therefore, all children) are. He holds them innocent and unaccountable for their sins.

I think it is critical to note here that it is not one's personal sin that keeps them from eternal fellowship with God, but the lack of atonement for that sin. God demands atonement for sin, and the only acceptable atonement He recognizes is the acceptance of His Son, the Lord Jesus, as one's Savior. Since children under a certain age are unable to understand and accept that gift of atonement from the Father, it follows that God does not hold them accountable.

To conclude otherwise is to put scriptures at odds with each other, and that would not be rightly dividing the word of truth. The most important rule of proper exegesis is that an interpretation or conclusion should never, never, never cause a portion of the Scriptures to conflict with another.

Finally, we have Old Testament confirmation of this teaching that children are held in innocence in the eyes of God. In **Deuteronomy 1:39**, we read, "Moreover your little ones . . . and your children, which in that day had no knowledge between good and evil, they shall go in thither, and unto them will I give it, and they shall possess it."

The Lord, through His prophet, made reference to a time when the children of the people had no discernment over right and wrong. And yet, the promised land was realized by those children. For the New Testament Christian, the equivalent promised land is eternal life in heaven, and it is reasonable to assume that children who today have no knowledge of good and evil are as "safe" in God's mercy as were the children of the Israelites.

Another reference is **Isaiah 7:16**, where reference is again made to an age of innocence. It states: "For before the child shall know to refuse evil, and choose the good. . . ."

If you are still unconvinced, please consider the words of a man who towered over the rest of us in terms of wisdom and allegiance to God: David. In **2 Samuel 12:23**, the prophet records David's considered words and sentiment following the death of his and Bathsheba's child. David said, "But now he is dead, wherefore should I fast? can I bring him back again? I shall go to him, but he shall not return to me."

This was not David's sorrow speaking. It was not just David's hopes and sentiment. It was the word from God. David knew the Lord intimately and personally. He was heaven-bound, and he was sure that his child would be there waiting for him. Can there be any stronger evidence that children within the range of the age of innocence are safe under God's grace; that there is, indeed, for lack of a better term, an "age of accountability"?

So, the only question that remains is, what age is the age of accountability? My personal opinion is that the actual age is arbitrary. The age probably varies depending upon a variety of factors (i.e., maturity, parental influences, exposure to faith, etc.). My children, because of the strong influence I had as a Christian parent, acknowledged their need for Jesus at very young ages. In another home, where that influence may not be present, the age would undoubtedly be higher.

I think it would suffice to say that the age of accountability occurs when a child knows the difference between right and wrong and chooses to do wrong despite that knowledge. At that moment, they become accountable for their own sin.

Now then, I wanted to bring this matter to your attention purposely on this day of devotion, because many of you have children who are under the age of accountability. Your approach on this matter with children must be customized to their specific age-group.

Lacking any background knowledge on your family, I would be remiss to offer specific advice to you in this matter. But generally speaking, you ought to be able to discern where your child stands in terms of innocence and accountability and tailor this devotion to meet their needs. As usual, I will provide a suggested script to use, but it will be written with children who have probably grown beyond the age of innocence. If you have younger children, you might want to speak to the topic of goodness with their spiritual needs in mind.

All of the above has been offered in addition to the actual lesson on goodness, which follows. I felt it important to either equip you with or remind you about this situational truth regarding the ability of children to discern good and bad. There is nothing more important than our children, and we don't want to leave anything to chance when it comes to helping them grow into "good" people.

I want to use **Mark 10:17–18** for a springboard into this topic. It may not be a perfect fit, but I think it affords us a good start to this lesson. These verses, speaking about Jesus, read:

And when he was gone forth into the way, there came one running, and kneeled to him, and asked him, Good Master, what shall I do that I may inherit eternal life? And Jesus said unto him, 'Why callest thou me good? there is none good but one, that is, God.

I have tried to master this technique of the Lord to disarm those who try to trip Him up by turning the tables on them and asking them a more difficult question. He did it so easily and so cleverly. And what He was really doing was deferring their question so that He could make a very important point that they needed to hear.

In fact, this was a point we all needed to hear. Jesus said that there was no one who was good except God. And not only is God good, but everything He does is good, as well. Sometimes we humans blame God for the bad things that happen in this world:

- A house burning down
- An automobile crash
- A pet dying

However, if we take Jesus at His word, and we should, then we know that God never makes bad things happen. House fires are usually a result of carelessness by someone; vehicles crash into each other because of drivers' inattention (due to texting while driving); and living things get old and die. It is life and all that goes with it that causes bad things to happen, not God.

- ☙ God is good.
- ☙ He is good constantly.
- ☙ He does good things.
- ☙ He always does good things.
- ☙ He desires nothing but good for us.

Now, admittedly, God will sometimes use the bad things that befall us to make good come from them, but in no way did He cause them to happen.

We know this from **Romans 8:28**, which says:

> *And we know that all things work together for*
> *good, to them that love God. . . .*

There are a thousand stories that both you and I have heard where this has been proven true. One that comes to mind is the account of the man who was in a big hurry but was held up by a flat tire. He was beside himself with frustration and flippantly spoke out and said, "Why now, God?" as if to say that he felt God was to blame. God was not to blame. His worn-out tires were. Had he spent a little more time looking over his vehicle, he would have realized that he needed new tires.

But God used that bad thing to bring about good. At the same time, He answered someone else's prayer. As the man lifted the flat tire to put it in his trunk, a flash of light caught his eye from the nearby woods. The sun had shined on the mirror of a vehicle in the woods and into his eyes.

He thought something looked wrong, so he walked a little closer to the woods to see if he could determine what it was. As he looked around, he spotted the tracks of a vehicle in the mud, a broken-down fence, and a few small trees snapped in half.

Realizing there had been an accident, he ran down to the vehicle, only to find a young woman trapped and crying. She had been there for hours. She had fallen asleep at the wheel in the dark hours of the morning and veered off the road into the woods. She said that since she awoke, she had been doing nothing but praying that God would send someone to help her, and He did.

That woman knew whom to give credit to. She knew that God had answered her prayer and used this man's unfortunate flat tire to effect a rescue for her. We aren't told with certainty, but it appears she blamed herself for the accident and not God. But she readily and rightfully gave Him the credit for saving her life. She knew that good things came from God.

James 1:17 confirms her sentiment:

Every good gift and every perfect gift is
from above, and cometh down from the Father
of lights, with whom is no variableness, neither
shadow of turning.

Every good gift, every good thing in our lives, comes down to us from God. Only God is good, and only God visits good upon us. He never gives us evil or bad.

How can I make such a bold statement? How can I be so emphatic? Simply because of what the second part of this verse tells us. God is the only constant in creation. What He says, He will do. What He promises will come to pass.

And we are told here that God gives us good. He never varies. He doesn't give us good and bad. He gives us good and good and more good. His will and His purpose is to be the good Father to us, to shower us with good things, not bad.

And there is no shadow of turning with Him. Any way you look at God, He is light; there is never a shadow. He is the Father of lights. He is light. And light is the opposite of darkness. Good is the opposite of evil. God is light and He is good.

And all that light and all that goodness God brings to focus on us. We are His prized creation, the only creatures who were made in His image. He desires nothing but good for us. Yes, bad things come into our lives. We must sometimes endure the effects of this sinful, woeful world (i.e., illness, pain, loss of loved ones, etc.), but those are the evils that this world give us. They do not come from God.

Pet loss for adults, but especially for children, can bring us to near emotional paralysis. It can be, and often is, one of the most traumatic experiences in their young lives. It can literally be life-shattering for them.

To help a child cope, and frame their pain and sorrow in the proper context, we need to talk to them about the goodness of God. We need to talk to them about how God can bring good from bad. Please do not underestimate the impact this can have on a child. In their limited awareness of the world and all its workings, there is one assumption that is universal with children: They believe in God. And in their tender little hearts, they perceive Him correctly as being good.

Explaining to them that God is not responsible for the bad

that happens, like the loss of a pet, and that He can make good
come from the bad the world gives us, will have a profound impact on their faith and their personal outlook on life.

What to Share with Your Child

*Let's start out this evening by asking a few silly questions. Just
raise your hands if you want to answer "yes," okay?*

- *Who likes it when something bad happens to them?*
- *Who likes to stub their toe?*
- *Who likes to get stung by a bee?*
- *Who likes to get bullied on the school bus?*

*Well, no one raised their hand, so I guess no one likes bad
things to happen to them. And I can tell you that I never want
bad things to happen to you, either. I am your mother (father),
and I love you, and when something bad happens to you, it happens to me, too.*

*You know who else doesn't want bad things to happen to you?
I know you know. It's God. God wants only good things to hap-
pen to us. But He knows that bad things do happen in this world.
So He tries to send us good things to help us with the bad.*

*Let me read **James 1:17** to show you how God sends good things
to us, and then I want to share a true story with you, okay?*

***James 1:17** says:*

> *Every good gift and every perfect gift is
> from above, and cometh down from the Father*

*of lights, with whom is no variableness neither
shadow of turning.*

Wow, this is amazing to know. Every good thing in this world comes from God. Even when I do good for you, it is because God is leading me to do it through my love for you. And nowhere does it say that God is the cause behind bad things. He isn't. Bad things come from the world and the devil and even other people.

Now for the story I promised you. I think you will find this story very, very exciting. This really happened, and you can see God working to help someone.

A man was in a hurry to get somewhere, but he got a flat tire and could not get there. He was not happy and he complained out loud to God a little. He kind of blamed God for his trouble. We all do that sometimes, don't we?

Well, as the man was finishing with fixing his tire, he spotted a reflection in the woods. As he walked over to see what it was, he saw a car that had crashed out of sight from the road. He ran up to the window, and there was a woman inside. She had fallen asleep while driving and crashed off the road and into the woods.

She was so happy to see the man and to be rescued. But do you know what she said? She said that the accident was her fault, not God's, and that she had been praying to God all morning and she was so happy that He had rescued her.

Wasn't that a great story? It shows how God can take a bad thing like the man getting a flat tire and not getting to where he was going on time, and make something good come out of it.

I think you kids know that in this life bad things happen. They happen to everyone. Some are worse than others, but bad things happen to us all. But God comes along and does good things to help us.

The death of Buddy was a bad thing for us. It hurt us to have to let him go. But from that bad thing, God has given us good. We have learned a lot of good things:

- 🐾 *We have learned more about God's love for us.*
- 🐾 *We have learned to have joy even when we are sad.*
- 🐾 *We have learned that God loves Buddy, too.*
- 🐾 *We have learned that Buddy is not gone, but just gone on ahead.*
- 🐾 *We have learned that Buddy is young and well again.*
- 🐾 *And we have learned that we will see Buddy again someday.*

This knowledge and hope are some of the good things that God sent to help us. He keeps His Word and promises to us.

In closing tonight, let's try to imagine what Buddy looks like right now. Let's talk about these questions:

- 🐾 *Is Buddy young again?*
- 🐾 *Does he still have that limp in his back leg?*
- 🐾 *Is he still a little overweight?*

Chapter 21

DAY 7 DEVOTIONAL: FAITH

T he seventh element of the fruit of the Holy Spirit is *faith.*

> *But the fruit of the Spirit is love, joy, peace, long-suffering, gentleness, goodness, faith. . . .*
>
> —*Galatians 5:22*

This is the final day of our weeklong devotional. I hope these daily installments have been helpful to you in helping your child deal with the grief your family is feeling over the loss of your beloved pet. I also hope that you have decided to begin holding daily Bible devotions with your children. Nothing will strengthen a family more than making time for God in your lives together.

Our word for today's devotional is *faith.* Here is a word that presents us with a quandary—or perhaps it solves one, I am not sure. In these modern times, if you try to speak to someone about religion, you will find them generally unreceptive. They usually shut down any conversation by saying something like, "Sorry, I never discuss religion or politics with anyone." And that might be a sound strategy, given all the cults and occult groups trying to recruit converts these days.

If, however, you were to approach that same person to talk about *faith*, they are more inclined to speak to you on the subject. Somehow the world views this word as more palatable. And yet, for all practical purposes, the words mean the same thing to most people, at least on the surface. Thus, the quandary I mentioned.

Fortunately, we do not have to make a distinction here, as the word that we will be discussing is *faith*. Even with this word you can find as many definitions for it as there are denominations who use the word to describe their beliefs. As usual, I would like to defer to the dictionary definition of the word to remove any bias.

That definition is this: "a confidence or trust in a person or thing." Another I found was "belief without proof." I kind of like both of those, but I have opted to provide you with my own. It may seem more simplistic than the others, but as we discuss it, I think you will agree that it accurately portrays what faith is. And this is my definition: "taking God at His Word."

It is direct, but simple. If we take God at His Word, we are doing both of the other definitions: We are placing our confidence and trust in Him and we are believing that Word without actual proof. And His Word tells us that:

- 🐾 He exists.
- 🐾 He created all that exists.
- 🐾 He created us.

🐾 He sustains His creation.

🐾 He sustains life.

🐾 And a myriad of other truths.

Accepting God at His Word is what faith is, and what it is all about. There is a Christian-themed T-shirt that I am sure you have seen before. It sports these words:

GOD SAID IT, I BELIEVE IT, AND THAT SETTLES IT.

I have to admit that it is pretty catchy, even cute. For a while that became the mantra for many Christians. Everyone was using the slogan. The words appeared almost everywhere: on T-shirts, billboards, television, the sides of buses, etc.

While I understood the meaning behind the words, however, I did not personally care for the slogan. I do not mean to nitpick or be harsh, but I found the words to be poorly chosen and faddish more than spiritual or biblical.

What does it matter whether I believe what God said or not? Why should my believing "settle it"? Shouldn't what *God* said "settle it"? Does it really change what God said if I don't believe it? The T-shirt should read, *GOD SAID IT, AND THAT SETTLES IT,* shouldn't it?

Okay, I'm off my soapbox now, and returning to our discussion of faith. I was trying to simplify our understanding of what faith is when I offered my definition of "taking God at His Word." That seems to sum it up. It is another way of saying, "from God's lips to my ears and heart."

God said it, and that settles it.

As much as I like the simplicity of my definition, however, I think we need to defer to the explanation that the Bible gives us about faith. It is a bit more complicated, but it is also much more powerful and potent. We find it in **Hebrews 11:1**, and it reads:

> *Now faith is the substance of things hoped for, the evidence of things not seen.*

If you are unfamiliar with this verse, your reaction might mirror my own when I first read it as a very young Christian many years ago. I eagerly read it, expecting some wonderful truth to be revealed, but the first thought that came to my mind was, *Whaaaaaatttttt?* I do not mean to be irreverent here, because I embrace the Bible as the absolute plenary, inerrant, living Word of the living God, and I now know that these words did disclose a wonderful truth.

But back then, this verse seemed like so much double-talk to me. Truth be told, it still holds some mystery and complexity for me. What peculiar words: "Faith is the substance of things hoped for." What on earth does this mean?

Well, that is kind of the point; from an earthly, or secular, point of view, the words make little sense. But from a spiritual perspective, they make complete sense. The things the believer hopes for are exactly those things that God promised us in exchange for our faith (i.e., eternal life; joint heirship with His Son, the Lord Jesus Christ; a crown of rejoicing, etc.).

What this verse is saying is that when God promises something, you can take that promise to the bank. It is as good as if it has already happened. Faith solidifies that hope and makes it the substance of God's promises to us.

If I haven't lost you with that, then it is just one more, short step for you to see that faith is the evidence of things not seen. All that means is that others can believe in the things not yet seen just by observing our faith. Our faith is the evidence.

In the book of Hebrews, God dedicates an entire chapter to laud the faith of several people from the Bible. He goes into significant detail heralding the wonderful ways that He used each of these personalities because of their faith. Nowhere in the Scriptures does He pay such a tribute to people who showed great love or who were gentle or meek.

Those are important attributes or attitudes for the believer to have, but nothing is more important than faith. Faith bridges the gap between man and God. Faith pleases God. He loves for people to take Him at His Word.

Taking God at His Word has a profound effect upon the human psyche. Faith is the enemy of doubt, uncertainty, unbelief, and fear. Those undesirable things take flight when faith takes up residence in our hearts.

Faith also gives us an inner strength that nothing else can. Do you recall the story that I shared with you earlier about Polycarpus, the bishop of the church at Smyrna? It was not so much courage that allowed him to stand and face his death by flames.

It was his lack of fear of what the world or men could do to him. Faith removes fear and doubt.

If you recall the words from **Revelation 2:10**, God told the believers at Smyrna: "Fear none of those things . . . be thou faithful unto death." Polycarpus didn't fear and he was faithful unto death. For him, faith was the "substance of things hoped for."

We all need to take God at His Word and trust what He says in every situation we face in life. In a time of bereavement like this, we need to trust what He says about the souls of every living thing being safe in His hands. And we need to pass along that trust to those in need of it most, our children. They need to know that God won't let them down. He keeps His promises. We can take Him at His Word.

What to Share with Your Child

Well, children, this is the last day of our seven days of devotions from the Bible. As I said earlier, meeting together like this and discussing the Bible and the help and good things that God gives to us has been very comforting. And it has also been good for us to meet together and to share the things on our minds and hearts.

In fact, it has been so good for us that we are going to try to continue taking a few minutes each evening like this to share with each other what we feel and what problems we may be facing at school or work. I want to know more about your day and what is happening in your life, and I want to share more about my life with you. There are probably some things I don't know about that I can help you with, and maybe there are some things you can help me with.

One thing I need your help with is for you to just set aside ten minutes each evening so we can meet like this. We will talk, look at a scripture verse, and pray. It won't take long, but it will help us to bond more closely and to be the kind of family we all want to be.

Now, today we are going to talk about the word faith. I think this is the best, if not the most important part of the fruit that the Spirit gives us, because without faith we can't really have any of the other things. We must believe in God before He can live inside us.

Okay, kids, so let me ask you, what is faith? Can you tell me what you think it is?

- 🐾 Give child(ren) time to respond. They will probably mull it over a little before they answer you, and they will more than likely say something like, "believing in God" or "knowing God loves me and will not let me be hurt." Both are good answers. Acknowledge their response in a very positive way so they feel that they are contributing. You want their time spent in devotions to be positive and something they look forward to.
- 🐾 Next, give them an illustration of faith. Children love to picture things. Here is an example story/illustration you might want to use.

Those answers were great, kids. But there is a little more that I want you to know. Let me tell you a story that might help us all understand better what faith is.

Let's pretend we were hiking out in the woods. We come to a fast-moving stream, and there seems to be no way across. But we really, really want to get across the river and continue on our hike.

There are some fallen-down trees lying nearby, so we gather them up and Dad and I lay them down across the stream and make a bridge.

It is kind of shaky and it bounces a little when I stand on it, but I am pretty sure it will hold us as we cross if we go across one at a time. I ask you if you think it is a good bridge, and you say, "Yes, it looks great."

So I go first. I cross the log bridge to show you it is strong enough to hold me. I get to the other side, and I turn around and call back to you to tell you to cross now. But you hesitate and then call back to me, "No, Mommy, I don't want to."

I call back to you and say, "It's safe. I made it across. You can do it! Don't you believe me?"

You answer, "Yes, Mommy, I believe you, but I am not sure."

Finally, after I talked to you for a while and made you feel safe, you stepped out on the bridge that I had made and you made it safely across. You wanted to believe me, but you just weren't sure, and when it came down to showing that you had faith, you had to fight away your doubts. And you did.

There seems to be no way across. . . .

Our faith in God can sometimes be the just like that. We believe in Him, but sometimes we just are not sure. Isn't that right? But faith isn't just believing God; it is taking Him at His Word and acting upon it. In the Bible, God tells us about all the great people who believed Him and the great things they did.

> 🐾 *Daniel did not fear when he was thrown in the lions' den. He had faith that God would protect him, and God did. And then God used him to be the boss over all of Egypt.*

> 🐾 *David was not afraid of Goliath, even though that giant was nine and a half feet tall. He knew that God would give him the victory, and God did. And then David became the king of Israel.*

> 🐾 *The Israelites were not afraid of the walls of water as they walked through the Red Sea. They knew God was holding the waters back and that they would be safe, and they were. And their enemies were defeated.*

All these people, and many more, put their faith to work. They not only believed God, but they did things to show their faith to other people. We can be just like them. Oh, we don't have to face hungry lions or giants, but we still face problems and pain each day. And God will help us, just like He helped the people in the Bible, if we let Him.

When Buddy died, it brought such awful pain and sorrow to our family. Facing that was as hard for us as it was for Daniel to face the lions. But we can show our faith the same way Daniel did, by not allowing ourselves to be afraid or hurt, by remembering that God is in control and that all is well with Buddy. We also know that we will see him again one day. Why? Because God told us we would and we are taking God's Word for that.

That is the end of our devotions for this week. We usually end by thinking about something about Buddy, but this evening I want to have a kind of review question. I would like for you to tell me two things you learned this week from our devotions. Could you do that?

Chapter 22

DEVOTIONAL REVIEW AND SUMMARY

It is customary, and perhaps even prudent, to provide a review and summation of important points following one's presentation. A review helps to remind the audience of important points and a summary leaves readers with a sense of the overall theme and purpose of the presentation. I will be very brief with both.

Because the target audience of our devotions were children, I thought it would be best to keep the daily devotions as uncomplicated as I possibly could. It seemed to me that using a different passage each evening would serve to congest the thinking of youngsters and that would be counterproductive. Revisiting one verse would ensure that their focus was not divided on a variety of different scriptures.

I wanted to use a portion of the Scriptures that provided multiple, yet related themes that I could expound upon on each of the seven days. The scripture verses would also have to be uncomplicated enough that devotions could be gleaned from them that would hold the attention of children.

I am sure there were other passages that I could have used, but **Galatians 5:22** satisfied my needs perfectly.

> *But the fruit of the Spirit is love, joy, peace, long-suffering, gentleness, goodness, faith.* . . .

I hope that you found the commentary and recommended presentations for your children uplifting, informative, and helpful. I especially hope that your children were impacted in a positive way by what they learned and have come to trust and rely upon the Lord in a much more intimate way.

If nothing else was gained, I pray that both you and your child understand that God does not bring bad things into our lives, only good. God often gets a bad shake from us humans in this regard, and I think it is important that we set the record straight and understand that His role in our lives is always positive.

I said that I would be brief and I meant it. I see no reason to revisit all of the points we covered this week. We just need to apply them and remember that these are the types of good things that God brings into our lives. There is nothing negative mentioned among the words we used from this verse. God is positive toward us, and despite the difficulties we experience in this world, we need to remain positive toward Him.

What to Share with Your Child

I hope that you will conduct your own review and summary of this week's devotions with your children. It is important to rehearse things with them so that they truly absorb the truths and embrace them. I am confident that you will, because if you have come this far in your reading, it is because your children's emotional and spiritual health is a high priority for you. God bless you for that. I wish all parents felt the same responsibility.

I want to leave you with something that might seem a little unorthodox. That is probably because it is. I want to provide you with a make-believe letter from a make-believe angel to your child. That hardly seems like the right thing for a Christian author to do, I know. It is almost like having children write a letter to Santa Claus.

Of course, I would not do that. But making up a letter from an imaginary angel might not be as bad as it seems. Children live in an imaginary world. They have imaginary friends. They hold imaginary tea parties with imaginary guests.

On some level, they know they are making things up, but for a child, the imaginary world is not only a way to escape to an adventure, but it helps them vent things that they ordinarily are reluctant to share with their parents.

Moreover, if you have a child who is distraught over the loss of the family pet, and you have tried everything to console them without much success, this could be the very thing that could make the difference. I have used this letter previously with scores of readers who needed help with their children's grief, and they reported to me that the letter worked wonders for the child's outlook. The letter may seem silly to you, but to your child it might be just what they need, a sort of "Peter Pan experience," if you will.

The bottom line is that I do not see how it could do any harm. If your child is old enough to question its authenticity, you can

explain to them that it isn't real, but that if an angel of God could
write to them, this is probably what they would say. Even if they
do not question the validity of the letter, you might feel more
comfortable doing that. In any event, when your child is older,
they will have come to the realization that the letter was imaginary and assign it the appropriate worth.

Before I violate my promise to be brief, here is my offering.
I have adjusted it from what I have sent others to reflect some
reference to the devotionals your child has participated in this
past week.

Dear (child's name):

*Hello. My name is Helper. This may come as a surprise to
you, but I am an angel and I live in the place the Bible calls
heaven. There are a lot of angels here, and we all have
different jobs to do. Mine is to write to kids and let them
know that their pets have arrived safe and happy here in
heaven.*

*One of the head angels told me that you were worried
about your "Buddy" and asked me to write to you about him.
I am very happy to do that. I don't know if you are old
enough to read this, but if not, I guess your mommy or daddy
will.*

*You will be happy to know that Buddy is doing just swell. I
know that he was very old and that it was hard for him to get
around back there on earth. I know that he had slowed down,
too, and he was always tired. I think maybe Buddy knew that
it was almost time for him to come here.*

But when he got here, he was not old anymore, and he

*wasn't tired and slow. In fact, I saw him just a little while
ago and he was running and jumping and having a great time
with some other dogs and angels. Isn't that great news?*

*I asked him if he missed you, and he told me (yes, he can
talk now—you will be so surprised by his sweet voice one day)
that he did, but that God helped him understand that one day
you would both see each other again and that made him very
happy. I hope that makes you happy, too.*

*Buddy misses you and hopes that you understand that he
had to come here, because he was getting so old. He knows
that you and your family have been having devotions this past
week and that you learned about love and joy and other
wonderful words from the Bible. He hopes you learned your
lesson on joy really well.*

*He knows you are sad that he had to leave, but he hopes
you now understand how to have joy even though you are not
very happy. I hope so, too, because when you see this place
someday, all the sadness you had back there on earth will be
forgotten.*

*Buddy says he will stay busy until the day that you come to
join him. He knows that you have some important things to
do in your life there, and he hopes that you will get busy
doing them, too.*

*Oh yes, he wants you to know a little about heaven, too.
He wants you to know that we do not have time here, no
watches or clocks. So, when you see each other again, it will
be like you were never apart, because no time had passed.*

*Also, he wants you to know that it never gets dark and we
never sleep here. It is just one long day here. He said to tell*

*you that everyone is so friendly here. No one ever argues or
says bad things. Everyone is happy and kind.*

*Well, I have to get going. I have a lot of other children to
write. But again, don't feel sad. Buddy is just fine. He misses
you and that makes him a little sad, but like in the devotions
you had, he has joy for being here, especially because he
knows he will see you again one day.*

Sincerely,
Helper